PROPERTY POWER

THE 49 **PRINCIPLES**

PETER ARMISTEAD

P
POWERHOUSE
—PUBLICATIONS—

COPYRIGHT

Powerhouse Publications
Suite 124. 94 London Road
Headington, Oxford
OX3 9FN

www.powerhousepublishing.com

DEDICATION

To my wife, Deborah Ross Armistead, and two amazing children, Gabriel and Sadie. To Mike and Dorothy Boggett. And to my second family, all the amazing people at Armistead Property.

CONTENTS

INTRODUCTION

If you're writing a book about real estate investing, really you need to be qualified to do so. However, there aren't any official qualifications to give you credibility in the business of real estate investing. Therefore, I am not a Master of Real Estate. That title doesn't exist. Yet, I do however have 20 plus years of real estate experience and accumulated knowledge that I would like to share with you.

I am a lifestyle entrepreneur. I have created a real estate business primarily to enable me to have a better quality of life. I'm not just focused on making the most money possible and empire building. Yes, money is a driving force for me, but it is not the sole or most important reason for doing business. I have a passion for doing business and for building properties, and I also have a passion for living a fulfilling life that has absolutely nothing to do with business and real estate.

I have created (with a lot of help along the way) an award-winning property business based in South Manchester worth many millions of pounds. I have an extensive property portfolio giving substantial passive income. I am financially free and don't have to work if I don't want to.

I am an outdoor enthusiast and a very committed father and husband. I live mainly abroad, in Whistler, Canada. I spend a lot of time in the mountains skiing and training for and running ultra-marathon races. I also love spending time at my off-the-grid cabin on an island just off the Canadian coast.

I make my job and my lifestyle dreams go hand in hand. Each of them enables the other to flourish. The result is a dream lifestyle for me.

Twenty years ago, none of the above was true. I was an employee working as a lawyer in London. I didn't have much surplus money. I worked all the hours I could and I didn't have much of a lifestyle at all. That all changed when I left the law in 2001 and set up my real estate business. Real estate is an amazing vehicle to achieve wealth and the principles contained in this book have allowed me to create and run a very successful business.

I was doing business before, during and after the worst property crash in living memory (2008) and the principles contained in this book have been tried and tested by me the hard way. I hope by reading this book you can learn things in a few hours, that took me years to figure out.

Thanks for reading.

POWER PRINCIPLE 1

ALWAYS FALL IN LOVE WITH YOUR PROPERTY

The investors' cliché goes that you should never fall in love with a property and buy it because you can see yourself living in it. Apparently, it's only amateurs who fall in love with real estate. It's the amateur investors who get all emotional, fall in love with a property, overspend, overshoot timewise and generally don't treat it like a proper business.

We've all seen the amazingly watchable Grand Designs, right? If you haven't, then this is highly-recommended property porn viewing. It's basically the same episode each week. An affluent family start building their dream home, spend way too much money and time on it because it's a labour of love, and in the end they are left with a project that doesn't stack up financially but is the most amazing, architecturally-designed masterpiece that everyone loves. A lot of property investors I know love rubbishing this approach. Well, I have news for you. I fall in love with pretty much every property I buy and I use this to my advantage.

Real estate is a deal-based business. It is a financial asset class and the figures need to work and stack up. If they don't, find a better deal and property where they do. However, if the figures do stack up, it's good that you do fall in love with the property. Never be afraid to show some emotions around your properties.

If I'm spending a few years of my life buying, developing and then, ultimately, selling a property, I usually develop a strong emotional bond with it. Over the years, I have worked out which are the properties with potential, which ones will develop up well and which ones will be desirable. I can see the potential before most people can and I tend to fall for some very ugly buildings that most people wouldn't touch. That's fine – as long as the building is as beautiful as it can be when we have finished our work, and the ultimate buyer falls in love with it as well.

I use the love and passion I have for a property as a positive force. Instead of just working on a property to make it better and to sell it for a profit, I go in hard with my work. I will tell everyone in advance that this is going to be the best development that we have ever done and that we are going to build the best property in the area. Then I work hard to make sure that we do what we have said we will do. I have a passion for hard work and for turning old, ugly buildings into beautiful ones, and this passion is 100% shared by my team.

We don't overspend financially and we don't overrun timewise on our jobs, but we do have the same passion and love that you see exhibited on Grand Designs. This is definitely a business advantage.

Now I didn't start off with this passion. I wasn't the kid who used to build houses with Lego blocks and knew that one day he wanted to become an architect. My passion for my work developed over time. I first started buying relatively modest, standard, terraced houses and apartments in South Manchester, 20 years ago. All I would do was give them a quick lick of paint and then tenant them or sell them on. At the start, I didn't really appreciate design or if I did it was very much a small factor in the process.

As we did more and more buildings, I started getting a sense of pride seeing the change we had made to a building. I also started getting compliments from neighbours or from tenants. About 15 years ago, a local building inspector for the council was giving us our Building Regulations Completion Certificate for a job we had just finished. He turned to me and said, "You've done a great job here, Peter. You've turned the worst house on the street into the best." It was a great feeling and that compliment has pushed me and my team to want to create better and better buildings. For me, a building isn't just a set of bricks: it's got the potential to be an amazing home for someone and it can stand there making an area look better for years after I've left this earth.

> **It's good to think on the same wavelength as your buyers. No one is going to buy a property from you unless they fall in love with it.**

Even though it should be a logical process to buy a property, it's always the heart that makes the decision first and then, later, it's justified by the head. Just look at the difference in prices for similar properties. In my area, you can buy a two-bedroom flat for £120,000 or you can buy the Rolls Royce job from us for £275,000.

To get the maximum price for your property though, you need to work hard and really go to work on every detail. Treat that property well, make it as beautiful as you can and give it as much character as possible. Inject your building with your passion, energy and love. If you are in love with a property, then the chances are that other people will fall in love with it to – and that means a sale.

POWER PRINCIPLE 2

DON'T WAIT TO BUY REAL ESTATE, BUY REAL ESTATE AND WAIT

I am often asked when the best time to buy real estate is and the answer (usually) is "now!" Let me qualify this by saying that if there is a real estate boom going on, it's probably best not to jump into the market unless you really know what you are doing as booms usually have a bust coming along very quickly after them. Also, if prices have been rising sharply for several years and then prices start to fall, again this is probably not the best time to start piling into the market. However, apart from a couple of obvious times, the general rule is: don't wait to buy real estate, buy real estate and wait!

In fact, I would go even further and say that it's so important that you start owning real estate as soon as possible, that it's probably a good thing to jump in *before* you are ready. If you were setting out on a journey, you wouldn't wait for all the traffic lights to turn green before you started out. Just make sure you have a good idea of your route and then start your journey.

> The benefits of starting your investment career early far outweigh the benefits you'll make by being amazingly well-prepared.

The skills and preparation needed will come quickly and along the way. In fact, they are generally best learned on the job anyway.

Start before you are ready and learn along the way. The important thing is to start building up your portfolio as soon as you can. Property is a great asset class and some of its best bits come when it has had time to mature. It takes time to build up a decent-sized portfolio with a good amount of equity in it. The first years are usually the hardest and the slowest, but then due to compounding as time progresses, your business increases exponentially – usually with you just doing the same amount of work.

If you have one house worth £100,000 and one year it goes up by 10%, then you have just made £10,000 of profit. If you have been in business for 20 years and had managed to buy one house a year (and that's way too modest a goal), then you could have 20 houses which have all gone up by £10,000. That's £200,000 of profit for very little work. The real work was done buying the properties.

I think of my portfolio like an orchard and my properties as my trees. I plant seeds as quickly as I can. I set them up in the early stages and tend to them. But after a while, they are pretty much growing by themselves on autopilot. Why settle for one tree when I can plant a whole orchard?

Real estate is best viewed not as a get-rich-quick scheme but as a get-rich-slowly business. Real estate tends to go up in value over time. Its capital value goes up and its income stream from rents increases as well. It doesn't always do so, it doesn't do so each and every year, and there are no 100% money-back guarantees here. But, as a general rule, as long as we have inflation and population growth that exceeds property building (as we have had for a very, very long time) then real estate will increase in value. In fact, historical trends show that it doubles in value every 7 to 10 years. This is where the amazing power of compound interest comes into play.

The sooner you get started, the sooner you can start enjoying the benefits of compound capital appreciation and increasing rents. Yes, there is good short-term money to be made, but it's the long-term money that is made from holding real estate that is usually the biggest factor in real estate wealth.

It's very important to grasp this as early on in your property investing career as you can. It's important not just to have a one-year, three-year or five-year business plan. With property, you should also have a 10-year, 20-year, 30-year and an eventual exit plan. I do, and all of the successful property investors I know do as well.

No one ever said, "I wish I'd bought that property 10 years later," but I've heard plenty of people saying that they wished that they had bought real estate earlier, or bought more of it. Plant seeds early and start with the end in mind. It's the same concept as paying into a pension pot. Everyone knows that the sooner you start saving, the better. I personally view my property portfolio as my pension pot. The more property I can get as quickly as possible, the better.

POWER PRINCIPLE 3

WORK SMART

Having focus and working smart are the very foundations of running a successful business.

As well as working hard, you absolutely need to work smart. Hard work without thought, focus and direction is misguided. You need to focus on results. Do not confuse effort with results. An hour spent working on the right thing is worth more than any amount of time spent working on the wrong thing.

Almost every successful businessman or woman starts with two beliefs: namely, that the future can be better than the present, and that they have the power to make it so through hard work and working smart.

> **Don't be busy, be productive.**
>
> **A relatively-short period of time spent working hard, and with serious focus, can put you many years ahead.**

It's very easy to go down a hole and start digging away, working hard but not really getting anywhere because, for example, there is no money in your chosen pursuit. A manual worker in a factory works very hard. However, he's picked an area that doesn't pay well and he's not working smart. He will never be rich or successful. This is also a common problem with many professionals and many business owners get stuck in the wrong sector. In recent years in the UK, the pub industry has been hit very hard by changing lifestyle patterns. People have been deserting pubs in favour of socialising in other ways and since 2001, 25% of pubs in the UK have closed down. It's a dying industry and I wouldn't want to try and make a living as a publican these days. It's much better to pick an industry that's obviously got a promising future.

You need to be very focused on channelling your efforts into areas that will produce you money. Real estate as an asset class has lots of areas that can make you some serious returns. It also has areas that are a total waste of time and are best be avoided. Focus on the areas that will make you money. I would advise that the subsidiary industries tend to make far less money than the main areas. So buying, developing, renovating, selling real estate all have some very good fundamentals behind them. Setting up a maintenance business, being a lettings agent, owning a cleaning company are probably less lucrative areas to get into. Best to focus first and foremost on the heavy-hitting areas as that is where 80% of your profits will come from.

As an entrepreneur you may have a natural tendency to always be looking for business opportunities and to be off chasing whatever shiny ball bounces into your path. However time is finite and no one has enough time to pursue everything that they want, so focus on the important money-making tasks you have set yourself and the key areas of your business. It is key to focus on getting results in the areas you have chosen, even if that means that you have to let some other profitable areas go. It's a price worth paying.

Apparently, Warren Buffett has a 5/25 Rule in Business (and this probably extends to general life goals and principles as well). He advocates writing out the top 25 things you want to do, with the most important at the top of the list. He then advocates striking the bottom 20 off the list, just leaving you with the top 5. This ensures that you are focused only on the most important goals and that you are not being distracted or spreading yourself too thinly with other less important goals.

I am always looking for where the money is and trying to assess if I'm working as smart as I can be or if I've missed a trick or a new area. Spending time working out what you should be working on is far more valuable to you than just jumping in and starting to work hard. Many times, people are working hard, but at the wrong thing. Working on the right thing is far more important.

During your process, you need to really be focused on the money before, during and after you have set out on a course of business. Where is the money in what you're doing? Will this make me money? Show me the money!!!

For years I used to have a Post-It sticker on my computer that said, "Will this make you money?" If I couldn't answer, "Yes," then I would stop doing what I was working on and I would refocus on what would make me money.

As you get more advanced with your investing and have more funds available, then you can look at a few more areas that may be good investments. This is the time to have a bit more of a look around for other opportunities – not before you have a very successful business in place. Never forget your true focus but, as time progresses, you can experiment. For example, developments are our bread and butter and the main focus of our business, but several years ago we set up a ground rents business. We also have a lettings agency now. These are natural add-ons to our business and legitimate business plans in their own right, but they were only established after we had reached a certain level with our developments and when we had achieved pretty much what we wanted to. Both these bolt-ons make money for us, are easy to operate and don't take much time away from our main business. They do not however come anywhere close to the profits we get from the main business we have of developing and renting properties.

POWER PRINCIPLE 4

RELENTLESS FORWARD PROGRESS

I have deliberately put this principle after Working Smart, and that's because working smart must come first. Once you have focused yourself and chosen your business plan, then it's time to go to work on it. Hard work and relentless forward progress are some of the main factors in how successful you will be in life and in property investment. They are not sexy or glamourous concepts, and this is very old-school advice that no doubt a lot of people won't want to hear, but this is the factor most linked to how much success you will achieve. Success is no accident – it is built on the foundations of hard work. You have to put in the huge amounts of work that will give you massive results and success, and constant hard work is one of the most important ingredients to the longevity of your business.

Bill Gates once stated that he never took a day off work in his twenties. He showed massive amounts of work. High achievement really doesn't require natural ability, luck or talent. There are no short cuts. It requires working your ass off. And when you do, great things happen. Now, I'm not saying that you need to work every single day for a decade like Bill Gates did. He was once the richest man in the world and a very extreme example of a person.

One of the best aspects about investing in property is its ability to generate passive income. The ability to receive a rental income stream month after month without doing much, if any, work is a great thing and is the goal of many/most property investors. However, you need to work hard especially in the early days to set up this system. You need to be working 12-hour days now so that you can be working two-hour days later on in life.

When you have established your niche and created your business plan, then you need laser like-focus to make this a reality. Don't be a dreamer. No one ever became successful by dreaming, only by doing and working hard. You need to focus relentlessly on what it takes to be the best in your niche. Don't look at too many different business plans. Pick one you like and one that makes sense and hit it hard, very hard.

You need a good amount of energy and hard work if you want a successful business. It's unlikely that there will be a Eureka moment in real estate, when you suddenly gain Facebook-style wealth. But if you slowly and steadily keep working, day in and day out, then wealth is very certain. Success is the sum of many, many small amounts of hard work and effort that, repeated, lead to success. You do need to keep working. Property is not a five-years-and-retire type of business. The longer you are in the game and working hard, the more wealth you will accumulate. Most of the investors who have been in the game for more than a decade have established very successful businesses with huge portfolios and massive net worth. It's almost unheard of to find a full-time investor who is just about getting by.

Don't think of property as a get-rich-quick business. It's best viewed as a get- rich-slow business.

> **Relentless forward progress is needed.
> Just keep moving forwards. It's okay to
> take a break, just never give up.**

I run ultra-marathons and specialise in races of 100 miles and over, lasting several days. One of the same principles which gives success in ultra-marathon races also gives success in the business world and life in general. This is the ability to keep going. There's an ultra-running cliche that says, "If you can run, run. If you can't run, walk. And if you can't walk, crawl. But whatever you do, you need to keep moving forwards." It's the same for business. You will make mistakes – lots of them. As long as you keep moving forwards, doing business and growing, you will be fine. Excellence and achieving your property business plan and goals is not an act, it is a habit.

Don't think of business as a straight linear line that slowly plods upwards. There will be ups and downs and, in any one year, you may take a step or two backwards. It's not necessary to win every single time. Even champions lose rounds. You will have "off" days and you will sometimes get sick and tired. But as long as you keep moving forwards, you will succeed.

This is partly because of the nature of business and success generally. It also specifically relates to real estate due to the compound nature of our business. An often-cited guideline is that real estate doubles over the long-term – on average, about every 7 to 10 years. This is roughly correct. If you had a portfolio of 10 properties worth £2,000,000 today and just worked on managing that portfolio efficiently for the next 10 years then, taking rough averages, it would be worth £4,000,000 in 10 years' time, (and this isn't even looking at the money that could be made on the rental side of things). Just managing to stay in the game pays dividends. Of course, just managing a property portfolio is probably a bit of an under-achievement. Working hard to increase the size of your portfolio, and to maximise the returns you have, will super-charge your rewards.

The bad news is that the hard work never ends. Every day, you should be working hard and learning new things to stay on top of your game. The good news is that the harder you work, the luckier you get and the more you enjoy your work. The journey is never-ending. Even when you have "made it" and achieved your goals, established a great business and (in theory) can sit back and enjoy the spoils, it really doesn't work like that. If you adopt the attitude of wanting to sit on a beach drinking margaritas, then you probably won't get there to start with. Each day, no matter what stage of your career you are at, you need to work hard and commit.

There are always at least two things waiting to trip you up in real estate. There are things that you do, to mess up. You will make mistakes; I have made many. There are also events that happen to you outside of your control. However, if you keep on going and persevere, even when things are deep and dark and you are in the hurt locker, you will be okay.

During the Great Recession of 2008–2012, things were bad in the UK and they were especially so for us. Back then, we had been in business for five years or so and were doing well. We had taken the step up from single units to larger projects and were not only getting quite good at our job, but we were making some good profit margins. However in 2008, the music stopped and everything changed. There was a worldwide banking crisis and this was especially acute in the UK real estate market. Banks stopped lending and wanted as much of their money back as they could get, as quickly as possible. The banks in the UK did everything they could to get money back in from the investors they had lent it to. Their very survival depended upon it and they were ruthless.

We had to work very hard on our relationships with the banks just so that they didn't force us into insolvency. In fact, for those four years we primarily worked not *with* the banks, but *for* them! Everything we did was focused on repaying them what they wanted while continuing to do business and improving our product. During this period, the banks really put the thumbscrews on us and it was almost impossible to do business. It wasn't anything bad to do with our particular business plan. (In fact, we had a great business plan.) We were in the midst of a banking crisis and the banks just weren't lending. The banks weren't able to do business any more and, without the banks lending and doing business, neither could the rest of us as developers need bank finance to operate.

As a result, all bar one developer in my area stopped building and looked for other areas to earn money in. Many developers left the game altogether. Some developers became estate agents; some set up maintenance companies. One developer I know left and set up a restaurant/bar and he's now happily living the quiet life in Wales pulling pints. Some even just accepted bankruptcy and moved on.

Can you guess what happened to the one developer who stayed? Yes, that's right, he got the living daylights beaten out of him for four long years! I know because it was me. That period was like a scene from the film, Rocky. You know the one: the scene right at the end when Rocky is in the ring in the final round, down and out, covered in blood, beaten half to death and then not knowing how to admit defeat, he drags himself off the mat, stands there and beckons Apollo over to him for a slap down.

Well, after four years of living that scene and getting a beating at the hands of the banks, finally in 2012, we had repaid them and were personally no longer in any debt to them or in any danger from them. They also started slowly but surely to recover, to increase their balance sheets and to start lending again. In 2012, it turned out to be not the end scene of Rocky I, when Rocky lost. It was the end scene of Rocky II, where he gets up as the last man standing, music blaring out, and hands raised in the air as the victor. We persevered, we worked hard, we did some great business during that period and in the end we were the last developer standing. All through the tough times we carried on building, each and every day. Even though it was hard, we carried on doing business, working with local suppliers, tradespeople and estate agents and making relationships that are still strong today and will last forever. We also had years to practise getting better at our craft and now our properties are the best in the area and our work the finest. By 2012, we were a battle-hardened, highly-skilled business and there was literally no competition.

POWER PRINCIPLE 5

KNOW YOUR CLIENTS
(THE BUYERS OR TENANTS)

As you start buying properties, you will get clients either in the form of buyers or tenants. You need to know the needs and wants of your clients and you need to give them what they want. There is only one boss and that is your client. Without them, you would have no one to buy or rent your product.

It seems obvious to say, but a home is such a big financial investment that a buyer isn't going to buy it unless they really want it and it meets their needs. Before you even start considering doing any renovation or development work (probably when you are at the buying stage), you need to be fully aware of who will be renting or buying your property when you have finished your work and are ready to sell or rent it. You need to know exactly who you are selling or renting to. This is especially important if you are doing any renovation work to a property and if you care about maximising your sales or rental prices.

There are many different types of clients out there, although they can be stereotyped to some extent. There are first-time renters, millennial buyers, serial renters, families, large extended families, low-income renters etc. We specialise in both rentals and sales to affluent millennials. Even though I am (unfortunately) not a millennial, I know this market well and I give them the property and the lifestyle they desire.

We know that our end buyers love old Victorian properties with character but that they do not have the time, patience or sympathy for the negatives of this style of property. They do not want to deal with damp, they don't want leaky sash windows and, even though they like a bit of outdoor space, they certainly don't want to spend their hard-earned leisure time mowing the lawn. Millennial buyers have a very different mindset to a person in their fifties or sixties who is quite happy and willing to accept some negatives as part of their property package. Millennial buyers want the full package and as little maintenance as possible. So we give them what they want – and they, in return, give us what we want.

Our buildings are usually lovely, old, Victorian buildings externally, but inside they are high-end, modern, cutting-edge, well-designed apartments. There's under-floor heating, granite work tops in the (fully fitted out) kitchen, lots of light and clean surfaces and every single feature is brand new. We usually use oak flooring throughout, we use floor-to-ceiling windows to allow in maximum light, the walls are always slightly off-white, the bathrooms have designer tiles and modern fittings.

In fact, these days pretty much every development/renovation we do is back to brick, ensuring that there is almost no maintenance going forwards for the new buyers. This is a real selling feature for our clients. We respond to what they want and give it to them.

We provide nice gardens and amenity spaces for the buyers and we keep hold of the legal title to the freehold and management company so that we can maintain the communal areas, leaving our buyers free to spend their time on more productive things. We make it clear to the buyers that we are a professional operation and that if they buy a property from us, they can rest assured that we will maintain the externals to the highest standards and that in 5, 10, 20 years' time it will be looking as good as it does today. This is a massive selling feature for us, and I've lost track of the number of properties we have sold purely because this one factor is so important for our target market. And, of course, we charge a fee and make a profit for all of this.

Different clients will want different things and it's not always obvious what they want. Working out what your client wants is a process that we went through. In fact, it's a process of continually learning. You personally should aim to meet your buyer/renter and talk to them. Be upfront and ask them (or find out from the agent) what they liked or didn't like about your property. I ensure that our instructed agent sends me a (brief) report on each viewing that takes place saying what the feedback is and what factors the viewers liked or didn't like.

On the next property we work on, we will continue doing what they like and what has worked, but we will especially focus on what they didn't like and change these areas. We will change these instead to things they will like.

On one of our jobs, for example, it became clear that single women were a bit put off by ground-floor apartments as they were concerned about potential crime. So, in our next job, we installed alarm systems. Several viewers commented on this as a positive and we sold ground-floor flats to several women. Now, we fit alarms as standard.

We also received feedback once that the dishwashers were too small and they should be full-size ones, so in our next jobs we will installed full-sized ones. It's not rocket science. It's just responding to what the client wants.

I find that the easiest way of working out what the client wants is either to ask them or, if they tell you first, then to listen to them. Spend time with them, get to know them and their needs. Spend a lot of time talking to your customers face to face. If you really want to know what they want, then ask them. Don't assume you know.

By knowing what the client wants, we are able to give it to them. We don't want to waste the world's resources (or our profits) by providing them with things they don't want or need. We want to get it right and give them what they want. We care about our client's needs: it's part of our business plan. You need to make it a very easy decision for them to buy a property from you.

POWER PRINCIPLE 6

PICK A SPECIFIC GEOGRAPHICAL AREA

Pick a geographical area, and an area of business, and become the expert in this area.

It's very hard to be successful in lots of different geographical areas. I find it's best to specialise. We picked a few geographical areas in South Manchester (M21 and M16 postcodes) and we focused on them with laser-like precision.

Aim to know as much as you can about your chosen area. You really can't know too much. You want to be the go-to guy or girl for your area or property type. You want to be the person that the agents call first when a certain property type comes on the market in the area you are operating in.

If you spread yourself over too wide a geographical area, or over too many different property types, you will be missing a trick. You need to be "the" (or at least "a") local expert.

Real estate isn't global or national, it's local. It's always a bit misleading when the property indexes say that the real estate market is falling or rising. That's fine if you are investing in some national REIT, but most of us will own individual properties situated in very specific and unique areas. And you need to know exactly what is going on in your particular area.

If you were investing in an area where the main employer is about to go bust, then you'd want to know about it as it could have quite a negative effect on your investments. And it's not just the big, headline-hitting things (like an employer relocating) that you need to be aware of. You need to know as much as possible about your area. We only operate in a couple of postcodes in the South Manchester area. It's an area that houses 30,000 people. I have set out to make myself the expert in these two areas and as we only operate in a couple of postcodes, we are able to know a lot about those postcodes. Now, I don't prop up the local bar and gossip about what the neighbours are doing. I'm not that type of local expert, but I do know a lot about the properties there. I know which are the good streets to live on. I know which are the rough or bad streets. I even know which are the better parts of the street. I know where the restrictive covenants are. I know where the underground streams are (which make it more difficult to do any basement work). I know which are the best bus routes into the centre of Manchester. In fact, I try to know as much as humanly possible about each house, on each street, in each postcode that I invest in. This gives our business an amazing competitive advantage against other developers, especially ones that are new to the area.

About 15 years ago, a development was done by another developer in one of my chosen postcodes: (M16) Whalley Range. It's a mixed area. It's got some of the best properties in Manchester, some massive lovely 200-year-old mansion blocks on beautiful, old, tree-lined roads. The area has also got its fair share of social problems. Thirty years ago, it used to be something of a drugs supermarket and home to some of the most notorious gangs in the UK. Those days are mainly behind it, the area has been gentrified and it is now quite a desirable place to live ... on the whole. There are still patches that are a bit rough and ready, and caution is needed when buying there.

So when I was offered a chance to buy a development opportunity on one part of a particular road, I declined. I knew that patch well, and I knew it was too rough, and sales prices would be capped at too low a level for us. I'm talking about the 200 yards either side of the actual development site. There was one bench in particular that I knew. The local drug dealers and takers would go there to buy and sell their products. It was 10 yards away from the development. So I passed on the opportunity and another developer bought the site and developed it. He eventually sold all the flats there, but the prices were very low and it was a hard, long, drawn-out process for him. Even today, 15 years later, that bench is still there and it's still serving the same purpose. Re-sales of flats in that development are about 50% of what they would be if it was just 300 yards away.

There are many benefits with choosing one specific geographical area. Three of the biggest are:

1. You get to be the local expert. People see you in and around your area doing business year after year and you become the local expert and the go-to investor there. You become a big fish in a small pond. Agents will know you, as will other investors who are also doing business. They aren't just competition: one day you will be buying their properties and doing deals with them.

2. You get economies of scale. We are the biggest landlord in our chosen area. We have roughly the same number of properties that any given high street lettings agent has on his books. Each year, we spend hundreds of thousands of pounds on building supplies with shops in the local area. This enables us to negotiate some very substantial discounts with a lot of the local suppliers. When we got above 50 or so properties, it became more cost-effective for us to employ our own lettings agent, rather than outsourcing it. In fact, the year we made this change, we saved nearly 50% on our letting costs. We also now have several full-time maintenance personnel, so we can avoid paying overheads and surcharges from agents etc. We wouldn't be able to operate like this and have these savings and efficiencies if our properties were scattered all about the country.

3. You save time. Many investors spend a huge amount of time travelling all over the country to find deals and/or managing their far-flung portfolio. Even if they have agents, they still have to spend time managing, sometimes, dozens of agents. As all of our properties are within seven miles of each other, our staff can easily get to them. We save time by having our properties close together, and time is money, after all.

POWER PRINCIPLE 7

PICK A SPECIFIC PROPERTY TYPE

As well as being very focused geographically, and on the type of client we are building for, we are also very focused on the types of property we buy and deal with. You need to find a property niche to specialise in. Even better, find something that you believe is missing in the market place – something that will give you an edge and will set you apart from other investors. In fact, this is the cornerstone of our "brand" and, in the age of social media, you really should have a brand. We aim to be the specialists for blocks of renovated flats in our chosen areas. We aim to be the "guys that do the flats".

Often investors who chase many different property types end up under-achieving on what they potentially could achieve. I see many investors buying properties in different areas (London, Wales, Manchester, Spain, Bulgaria) and looking at and buying different property types (detached houses, flats, HMOs, small commercial). Maybe they are actively and consciously employing the financial concept of diversification, but this is not as applicable to property investment as it is to the stock market and, in my experience, does not work as well as specialisation.

Property investment and development can be complicated and if you are trying to deal with too many property types, you end up becoming a generalist. You will end up as a Jack of all trades and master of none.

How can you know everything there is to know about new-builds, renovations, listed buildings, shops, light industrial, apartment blocks, HMOs (the list goes on)? It's impossible – but that's what many people aim to do!

We choose to specialise in blocks of flats, usually in old, Victorian buildings. Most investors in this property type are focusing on the low end of the market, but we saw that the higher end had huge demand but was very badly served. There were lots of affluent professionals choosing to come to South Manchester wanting to live in nice, smart apartments, but there just weren't the apartments there for them to live in. We could see people able to afford decent apartments, yet they were having to live in average ones, because there just weren't the stylish apartments around for them.

In short, there was high demand and low supply in this area. High demand, low supply is a great opportunity for a business and enabled us to operate in an environment where the business tide was in our favour. We saw an area that was underserviced. We saw an opportunity and a gap in the market. When limited supply meets excessive demand, there is always an opportunity.

Real estate is certainly one area where, contrary to popular advice on the benefits of diversity, I find that it tends to be better to put all of your eggs in one basket – as long as you make sure it's a great basket. Market specialisation is the key to success in property investment. It's been the cornerstone of our business plan and has worked very well for us.

We adopted this business strategy of specialisation 20 years ago. After a lot of research, I picked a specific geographical area (two postcodes in South Manchester) and a specific type of property, (blocks of flats), and started doing business purely in that area and purely with that type of property. We started off doing single apartments and terraced houses, then after a few years of doing these and learning our trade, we moved up to doing small blocks of four, five or six units. This was a good plan for a while and we did many of these blocks. For the last seven or eight years, we have been more focused on larger blocks of 12 to 20 units.

At first glance, you may think that this is a very limited and therefore flawed plan and that we were missing out on lots of other opportunities in other geographical areas and/or in different property types. And you would be right! I certainly have missed out on some opportunities. However, the benefits of being so focused on one particular niche has paid dividends many times in excess of what I could have achieved if I had not have focused so hard on that one area.

I got to know my targeted niche so well that I became the go-to guy in my area for that type of real estate. If the local agents get a block of flats, then usually I get the first phone call from them, quite often before it's even been listed and usually I manage to buy the property. I've probably bought most of the blocks of flats that have been sold in my area in the last 20 years. As time goes on, we get more properties and we do more work on and to them, and get even better at our job. Business becomes easier, not harder, as time progresses and the more practice you are able to have.

We have also become absolute experts at squeezing every last bit of value out of these types of properties. We can do far more with a block than another developer and hence can afford to pay more generous prices (as we know our profit margin will be higher), which in turn means we usually are successful in securing the property. We have been working on and developing very similar blocks for many years now, and even before I enter a building I know what the layout will be internally and what we can do to it.

It enables me to know exactly what I am doing and what I want to do. I can act quickly. If an agent calls me up with a potential deal, I can give him a "yes" or "no" on the spot. Chances are it doesn't even hit the local market, as I've snapped it up quickly before other investors have seen it. If I had to go and do my due diligence from scratch, it would be a longer, more drawn-out process, the property would probably end up on the open market and I would have missed any advantage of getting that phone call.

POWER PRINCIPLE 8

PICK AMAZING PROFESSIONALS AND WORK WITH THEM

As a property professional, entrepreneur and business owner, you will inevitably be a Jack of all trades. I wasn't a property professional until I was 29 years old and I have no formal property qualifications. This is absolutely no obstacle to building a successful business.

As an investor and developer, you need to have a very wide skill-set if you want to succeed. In the early days, no doubt you will be trying to do everything yourself. The traditional trajectory (and one I myself took) is that you become interested in and dabble with real estate when you already have a steady job that you are probably not really satisfied with. You find a property to buy which you think will be a good investment after many hours, days and weeks of looking and doing your due diligence. You negotiate the price. You go out and find the money (probably from your own or your friends' or parents' bank accounts) for the deposit. You arrange bank finance. You buy the property. You renovate it yourself using very cost-effective materials and doing the best job you can. Then you post an advert and rent it out. You manage the whole tenant-finding process yourself and you move a tenant in and then deal with them and the ongoing property management and maintenance. You are, in effect, trying to be an all-round general expert in property sourcing, negotiation, lettings, property management, property finance, building techniques and probably an amount of interior design as well! As your business progresses, and you do more and more deals, you should aim to firstly contract out and then eventually bring in-house as many of these jobs as you possibly can.

Firstly, when you contract these jobs out, find an amazing lawyer, an amazing estate agent, several amazing property sourcers, an amazing handyman and an amazing lettings agent. If picked correctly, these people will do the job way better than you can. Your time should be spent managing the experts you are using and running your business.

> "There's one amateur in my business and that's me." – Peter Armistead

Now it's easy to say, "Go out and find amazing professionals to work with," but in practice it can be quite hard to do. I personally have made bad choices (although not often) and when you do, it's blindingly obvious. Cut your losses early and don't deal with anyone you think is less than great. I would advise asking other property investors who they use and asking for recommendations. If you see the same names cropping up again and again, then it's a safe bet to use them. I usually find that there are certain lawyers/accountants/actuaries, etc., who specialise in dealing with property professionals. They tend to get one client, understand their topic, do a good job and then the next thing you know they are recommended by their client to another client. Sooner or later, they become a go-to professional for property investors. One of the first things I did when I started investing was to ask my mentor at the time who his lawyer was, and I started using him. I continued using him for the next 10 years until he sadly, retired.

When you scale up your business, you can choose to have these experts in-house as part of your team. It's vital to get a great team, as a team always trumps an individual in business. If you fail to instruct amazing professionals and try to carry on solo, you will be limited by what you can or can't do. It's true you can become quite successful just by being a one-man band, but you can never create a truly successful and scalable business until you are instructing people better than you to do your work. It requires more management of people and systematisation of your business from you, but the benefits will be massive. You can also choose at what stage you hire these staff and how you structure your business. Every business has a different emphasis and feel but the principle is that you should be working on your business not in it.

The first member of staff I employed full-time was a handyman. This was at the stage where we had about 20 to 30 properties. We bought most of them in quite a run-down state and I needed someone to do cheap and quick renovations on them and to generally deal with any maintenance that cropped up. (Maintenance and being handy is definitely not my strong suit!) After a year or so, it became clear that the scope of our building work was increasing quite rapidly and that the one handyman was overwhelmed, so I then hired two proper builders to do the work. A couple of years later, they too were overworked and I employed more builders and we did bigger jobs. A lot of property developers just contract out the building work. In fact, that is standard practice, but I decided early on that I wanted this side brought in-house, so that I could control quality, schedule and costs better.

The first property professional I brought on board was a property manager. When we had accumulated 50 or so properties, it was far cheaper to have my own property manager working full-time for me, rather than running them through a high street lettings agency. It becomes quite obvious which professionals you need, and when you need them, as your business grows.

And, of course, it goes without saying that the better the experts you can find and employ, the better your business will be.

CHOOSE GREAT DESIGN

Good design sells. It's that simple. Good design may mean different things to different people, but the general principle is that the better the design aspects, the more value your property will have. Some people may like old buildings and some may like new buildings, but good design goes to a bit of a deeper level than just a quick, aesthetic choice. Good design is not just about what looks good visually on the surface, it is also how a building functions and operates.

Good design in products, and especially in homes, has a powerful effect. Good design will create a visual connection with your client and, if done well, will alter their mood for the better. Good design also plays a very important role in many marketing strategies as people pay a premium for good design.

It's self-evident in many areas of life and especially so with property. Look at what Apple has done, or how many people choose to pay hundreds of pounds on trainers, when you can buy a similar functioning product for a tenth of the price. Never underestimate the power of design and never think that a person buying a house is buying a purely utilitarian product. Even if they do not know why they like something, if it's well presented and put together, buyers will pay more – and often quite a lot more. Everyone is influenced by design even if they don't realise it and even if they don't classify themselves as design- or style-conscious.

Many investors, especially those investing in traditional buy-to-let properties in the sub £250,000 bracket, do not fully appreciate and focus on the power of design. I see a lot of developers trying to make aesthetic decisions themselves or in conjunction with their friends or partners, who are not interior designers. The standards for, and emphasis on, good design in the buy-to-let market tends to be pretty low. Most investors are fanatically focused on the financial bottom line and have a mentality of firmly controlling expenses. It's a good mentality to have and you have to make sure that when you are doing any building work that the costs are controlled. Also, when renting a property you don't want to be spending thousands of pounds on amazing furniture if you're only going to get £500 per month in rental income.

However, I find that people are really missing a trick here and that money spent on cost-effective interior design has some of the best returns we make. I find that £1,000 well spent on good design can easily add £2,000 to £3,000 on to the price of an apartment. We often install some very smart kitchen counter tops using high-end quartz or granite, for example. We also use the same quartz for our windowsills and any internal ledges in the property. It's not a huge cost, but you would be surprised by how many people comment on and like this feature. It's definitely worth doing and, for a cost of just a few hundred pounds, it adds a few thousand to the overall sales prices of the flats.

You do however need to get it right. We certainly don't overspend, but usually I find that a few hundred pounds on something eye-catching and good quality is worth doing.

> **You need to get the best bang for your buck.**

Usually, it's not the expensive blinged up fixtures and fittings that we spend our money on. Rather, it's a skilful interior designer who knows what materials go well together. It's more about making the right choices (quite often with budget fixtures and fittings). I personally don't have those skills, but my wife and business partner does. If she didn't, then I would pay a quality interior designer to do the work.

Getting a skilled designer and paying their time costs is the most important part of the equation and you should spend time finding a good or great interior designer. They need to have an eye for how rooms and buildings work, feel and flow: how the light enters, where the doors are situated, how the kitchen is laid out. These are all choices that a skilled designer will be able to make without spending much money (if any) on dressings or fixtures and fittings. It's about making the right choices. You're going to be using tiles in the kitchen, right? You might as well get ones that match the kitchen counters and flooring in a well-considered way, rather than just hoping it works or, worse, not even caring. Design is about how things look and also about how they flow and work in practice.

When our business only had 10 employees, we had an interior designer and an architect working on the pay roll. That is how important I think design is.

The more expensive the property/development, the more important this principle is. Find a good interior designer, one who will work to a budget and then spend time educating them in your business plan and tenant profile.

POWER PRINCIPLE 10

THE "WOW!" FACTOR

> When someone walks through the door
> you want the first word to come out of
> their mouth to be, "Wow!"

The best properties have the "Wow!" factor. I find that the most successful developments we do are the ones where people walk through the door and are obviously moved by what they see – to such an extent that the first word out of their mouth is usually, "Wow!"

As a developer you need to hold yourself up to the highest standards in your field or, better still, to raise the bar and create standards better than your competition. Pay attention to the details. The most successful real estate projects result from developers paying attention to the hundreds of little details that are overlooked by their competition, but that are greatly appreciated by their target market. You need to make sure you are the best in your class.

Make sure you stand out: don't compete on price, compete on quality. We always start out the build process by working out what the range of prices are for the apartments we are building. We then look at the highest figure and we go in aiming to get the top end of the range (why wouldn't we?!). Then, we have months and months of work to do and many thousands of decisions to make to ensure that our properties will achieve the highest prices when they are marketed. And this involves creating the "Wow!" factor.

When a buyer is viewing properties, they will only buy one and they will buy the best one that they can for the money they have. You need to make sure that your property is the best one that they view. Don't make it the cheapest. I find that it's a self-defeating process to try and compete on price, as this will just destroy your potential profits. I would recommend competing on quality. Don't try to create the cheapest property on the market. Make sure yours is the very best property that it can be.

If your potential buyers always seem to be focused on the price, it's because you haven't given them anything else to focus on. You've not done your job properly. You need to be providing something else that they want. You need them to walk into one of your properties and be blown away by how amazing it is. The fact that it's also one of the most expensive properties around is now not that important. In fact, psychologically, sometimes the high price is appreciated as the buyer knows that they're getting the best quality property on the market.

It's not easy making sure that your property stands out, but this is your job and it's actually a very enjoyable part of the job for most people. You should ideally be working hard on the design of the property way before any renovation works are done and right at the earliest stage of the process. Choose your materials and fixtures and fittings carefully. Ensure that you employ builders who can build to the highest of standards, and especially with a really good quality finish, as this is what most people see and focus on (the plastering and the painting are some of the most eye-catching features of the property). Additionally, always make sure your property is clean, furnished and dressed well before you attempt to market it.

You are, in fact, a property disruptor and innovator – whether you know it or not. It sounds quite an outrageous claim when you're just investing in property, but that really is how I see myself and it's how a lot of the big developers see themselves as well. You need to be almost creating a new market place and giving people something they don't even know that they want yet. You need to be thinking about the future. As we focus on affluent millennials, we need to be asking questions such as, "Will our end users want (and be prepared to pay for): electric charging points for their cars; smart phone-controlled heating; underfloor heating? Will they pay extra for a well-maintained block?" Now, we are talking real estate here and you don't need to reinvent the wheel, but anything that you can do to make your product stand out and be better than the competition is great.

You can front-load a lot of your work here. When we had spent time finding the best suppliers, finding the best quality and best value materials etc., then we had a pattern that worked and could be repeated. We do change our pattern every few years to keep things fresh and better than the competition, but it's now small changes and tweaks to an established and workable pattern. A new type of kitchen, a new bathroom tile on the floor, better quality stone counter tops, bigger and better windows, larger balconies, better quality flooring, etc. We don't need to reinvent the wheel each time.

POWER PRINCIPLE 11

ANALYSE THE FINANCIALS IN GREAT DETAIL

Real estate is a numbers game. You have to have a clear, cold head when looking at a deal. If you want to have a successful business and to be rich, you need to focus on the figures. Everything I look at, everything I am doing, I'm looking at the figures side to it. Every single day, I will be analysing the financials in my business in some way.

The monetary side of property is the bottom line reason that most of us are in this business.

> Real estate is a great asset class, and a great business to be in, but you need to make sure you get your figures right.

You will need a good spreadsheet. There are lots out there that you can tailor to your specific property and project. You will obviously need to put figures in all the relevant boxes to work out if your deal is a goer or not. Make sure you get an expert to advise you on each box. The finance/mortgage broker will be able to give you a handle on the loan costs. The builder will be able to tell you the build costs. The estate agent will be able to tell you any potential re-sales prices, etc. Put all the figures in. Make sure both yourself and at least one other professional has checked and approved each main figure (build costs/loan costs/re-sales, etc).

Usually I get at least two opinions, as well as my own estimates, on the figures. I operate on a trust-but-verify policy in most of my business and nowhere is this more important than with the financials and deal analysis. If you are not a numbers person, then you are going to have to become one (or get a partner who is a numbers person) and you will have to work extra hard in this area. This is one area that you can't delegate out and it's crucial to the success of your business. You can afford to make mistakes on most areas of your business and you will survive. The cleaning company can mess up. You can miss an appointment here or there. Your builder can even do a bit of shabby work that you don't spot. Life and business will still generally go on. However, messing up the financials is one of the more serious mistakes you can make, so best to focus proportionately more time here.

It's also very good practice to underestimate sales prices, and overestimate the build costs. Build costs, especially with renovations, tend to be higher than the initial estimate as there are so many unknowns that can crop up when you start making changes to a building. New-builds are actually a lot easier to plan and manage.

It's tempting to massage your figures so that you make them fit a deal that you want to do. I've been guilty of this myself where I have found an amazing building that I've wanted to buy and work on, but where the figures just didn't quite stack up. The financials are a great reality check. The financials don't lie. If they don't stack up, don't do the deal and do not get caught up in "deal fever". If you are ever in doubt about a deal, look at the figures and they will tell you whether to go for it or not.

POWER PRINCIPLE 12

AIM FOR A 20% MARGIN ON OVERALL SPEND

Over the years, I have found a very good rule of thumb is that you should aim for at least a 20% profit margin. This means that you need to make 20% profit after all costs (apart from taxes) have been factored in to a job. If I can achieve in excess of a 20% margin, then the deal is a good one and I will buy the property. If not, you need the discipline to reject it and walk away. Of course, many of our deals give more than the 20% profit margin and it's perfectly possible to get up to 40% or even 50% returns. In fact, most of our deals are actually in the 30% to 40% return bracket, although we do have to work very hard to get those figures.

A minimum of at least a 20% profit margin is vital in ensuring a viable business opportunity. It is a good amount to ensure that your business actually does turn a profit and can grow. A 20% margin usually gives you such a decent return that you can take your personal salary from it and also have surplus to do more and bigger deals in due course. Less than a 20% margin can often mean that a business is pretty much just treading water. It may pay for your salary, but it doesn't enable you to expand and progress the business. You basically have a hobby rather than a business. You need to be doing deals that enable your business to grow and expand. You need surplus money, a decent profit margin.

A profit margin of at least 20% is also a good figure as a safety margin in case something goes wrong. If the market softens, you could see headline property prices fall by 10% or so, but if there is already a 20% margin in the deal then you will be safe and probably won't lose money. It's very rare that the market does fall 20% – very rare. The worst property crash in living memory was 2007 to 2009 and prices nationally fell 13% over this two-year period. You are very unlikely to find yourself facing the situation where the market has fallen by 20%.

It's more likely that the worst that will happen is that you will try to sell when the market is flat and very quiet, but prices technically aren't any lower. In that case, you can reduce the sales prices by say 5% to 10% and still make money or (probably, a better option) you can re-finance and get pretty much all of your money back out of the deal.

> **Ensuring that there is a 20% margin in a deal saves both your ass and your assets when a market turns against you.**

There are lots of 20% deals out there. Don't be rash and go for a deal that has a lower profit margin. This is the general advice when doing small/medium renovations and developments of up to 30 units. When you start getting over this level, however, the rules are different. As there is a lot more money at stake, the percentages tend to be lower. I frequently see larger developers doing deals with only 10% margins, but the overall numerical profits are that much higher. For example, 10% profit on a £50 million development is not to be looked down on.

Have the approach that there are plenty of properties and deals out there. You don't need to compromise on the bottom line. Soon, you will find a deal that does stack up.

When you first start networking – talking to agents, other investors, sourcers and doing your own searching online and walking the streets – do not be disheartened if you don't get a deal immediately. The cumulative effect of all of these efforts will pay off and there are plenty of deals out there if you stick with it. Stay the course and do not be tempted to settle for deals with less than a 20% return.

POWER PRINCIPLE 13

FRONT LOAD YOUR WORK

I find that the most important and financially-rewarding work is what we do between buying a property and actually starting the building work. It's the time spent discussing strategy, looking at planning options, working out what potential the building has, maximising value and going through the building regulations process. It's the time spent looking at what we can get out of a property and looking at the different layout options. This is the design and planning phase and is the phase that I personally spend a lot of my time working on. This phase takes about four to six months for most of our projects, compared to 12 to 18 months of build time. This is the phase when the most profit per cost can be achieved and, if done well, it can supercharge your profits. Typically, 30% of our profits can be achieved before we have even started building by some good design work and especially by a good planning uplift. Planning uplift is key and getting good planning permission really is one of the most important parts of the job.

It's definitely worth finding a good or great architect and spending as much time with them as you can discussing potential plans, layouts, numbers of rooms, number of units and general options for your property.

Typically, for new investors, this is the stage where they don't know what they don't know. Most investors tend to be out of their depth here. I certainly was for the first few years of my career. Don't worry if you find yourself a bit overwhelmed here for a period. It is just the natural progression of the property investor's career path.

Planning is a very complicated area. I've read pretty much all of the books out there on planning and although some are good ones, none of them give you what you need to really maximise your building's potential. A book, a course, or a podcast isn't good enough here. This is one area where you really do need the best expert you can find. Yes, you should have a good general overview of what you can and can't achieve with a property, and this knowledge is crucial at the buying stage. But when it's time to sit down and start talking about a detailed submission to the planners, this is where you need to give instructions to a good architect and/or planner.

Whereas a developer/investor may make only several planning applications a year, a good architect or planner will have made hundreds, will know what can and can't be achieved with a building and will know how to go about the process in the best way, which isn't always just submitting an application. In the best cases, the architect or planning consultant will have good personal relations in the local planning department, enabling him or her to pick up the phone and talk directly to their contacts to see how a set of potential plans will be received by the planners at the council.

This is not to say that you should blindly follow the architect's advice. You too need to commit to spending time and energy on this area. You need to spend time learning plans, room layouts, ways of maximising space. There are no shortcuts here. As the developer, the buck stops with you and you need to get it right. In my chosen location of South Manchester, the difference between a one-bed flat and a two-bed one is roughly £80,000, yet costs only an extra £10,000 to build. It makes sense to spend time focusing on increasing the number of units you can get or the number of bedrooms, etc. As a developer, this is one area that you really need to focus on. You can't just delegate it, it's vitally important that you get to grips with it.

Many investors and developers jump into jobs with scarily vague plans and then change them, for better or worse, as they are building. This is NOT the way to go about a development and, quite frankly, is just laziness. Yes, you should always be on the look-out for extra space as and when you are building and also any potential improvements that can be made, but do not think you can skimp on the design phase.

You want to spend so much time perfecting your plans for the property that when you start building you can almost just give the plans to the builder and say, *"There you go. See you at the end of the job,"* as all the relevant information is there and you have spent so much time on analysis and planning that you have done all you can.

I find that the correct time to have a near-perfect set of plans is actually just after the demolition/strip-out phase. The chances are that you have a set of plans that you have secured planning permission on. You now need to get these fanciful works of art into the real world and create a set of plans that your builder can build to and that will pass building regulations at the end of the day.

I like my builders to go into a property for a couple of weeks to strip out a good amount of the old stuff. When we have done some basic stripping out, we will then be able to see some key bits of the structure that will no doubt change the way we are contemplating building. We need to see which way the joists run, how big the purlins are and exactly how much head height we have. Once the architect has all of this information, we can get a set of plans ready for submission to the building inspector, and also to be given to the builders as well. Don't try to give them a final set of plans before you have stripped out, as this phase is always a bit of a game changer.

Typically, I will spend 80% of my time buying a property and on the design stage, and 20% maximum actually on site, during the course of the build. It used to be more like a 50/50 split. But as I get more experienced, I know that the more time I spend on the design and planning stage, the better the job will be overall, and the less time I will spend in total on the actual project.

EITHER BUY BELOW MARKET VALUE OR WITH A POTENTIAL UPLIFT FROM DEVELOPMENT

I never start the deal-finding process by going out and looking for lovely properties. Instead, I look for people that want or need to sell or focus on ugly, distressed properties that are being badly managed, where we can add value. You are almost never going to find a nice fully-renovated and well-run property that the seller will accept 80 pence in the pound for. Yes, these deals do exist but they are rare as hens' teeth.

Usually, if you find a deal like this they tend to be packaged up by property sourcers (professional property finders who specialise in finding deals for investors). If you are handed such a juicy deal on a plate by a sourcer, you need to first of all ask yourself why they are offering you such a great deal and why haven't they either taken the deal themselves or offered it to their brother or close friend? Why are you the surprise recipient of this good fortune? You need to do a serious amount of due diligence here to make sure that all of the information you have been given is true.

Usually, properties that are either being offered Below Market Value ("BMV") by sourcers or that you have found and appear to be BMV have a twist to them and involve a lot of hard work to realise the profit margin. When you have worked out what the twist is and what the work is, you can breath a sigh of relief. You're not being conned by some imaginary discount. You have found a deal and a property where you can make money.

I have bought and sold over 500 properties and I have made a profit on every single one. Not one of the properties was a perfectly well turned out property that I could immediately sell for more the day after I'd bought it. All of them required brain work and hard work to get to the profit. That's fine. That's the game we are in. We buy, renovate and sell property.

I have found that many properties out there genuinely were below market value, but they all needed at least some work doing to them. Usually, they need a lot of work doing. It's great looking at properties and finding a property £50,000 below the last comparable sale. But if you need to spend £50,000 renovating it to get it to this standard, there is no profit margin to be made. You can make a very nice amount of money with property, but don't expect pre-packaged BMV deals to do this for you. It's never that easy. If it was, then everyone would be doing this.

Quite often, when a property requires renovation or development work, there is a potential profit margin to be made. These are the deals where I have made most of my money. I usually find that the more work involved, the bigger the potential profit margin.

> **There is usually no such thing as money for nothing in real estate.**

As with everything in life, you will need to work hard to gain the profit. I find that things of value and importance are usually only gained by massive amounts of work and this is certainly the general rule with property as well.

POWER PRINCIPLE 15

BORROW MONEY AT ONE RATE OF RETURN, INVEST IT AND MAKE A BETTER RATE OF RETURN

Property Investment, and investment in general, is all about borrowing money at one rate of return, investing it and making a higher rate of return. This is the general principle behind all business ventures and it is the same in the real estate asset class.

You should aim to keep your borrowing costs way below your anticipated profit margin. If you can borrow at less than 10% and are making over 20% returns, then it's a viable deal and you should jump on it. Both of these figures need to be constantly reviewed.

> **Aim to get your borrowing costs lower and your profit margins higher.**

It's also important to work out what you are able to borrow and what profit margins you need to make. Both these variables go hand in hand.

On some properties I've borrowed at 5% interest rates and have made a modest profit. On some properties (usually the larger developments we do), we can afford to borrow at 20% as our profits have far exceeded this amount.

Understanding what you can borrow, and how, is key to property investment. In the early days of a property investor's career when an investor is learning their trade, the investor may have one or two different financial strategies available to them that they use successfully. We certainly did back when we were starting out. We used standard buy-to-let mortgages (pre-2007) at around a 5% interest rate to buy small apartments that were generally undervalued. Then, later on, as our business increased in size and became more sophisticated, we branched out and started using different sources of finance.

Most medium to large property businesses will have several sources of finance that they can access. We have joint venture partners, we use bridging companies, we work with commercial banks, buy-to-let lenders and private individuals. All of these sources of finance will want different returns, will want to lend in different ways and will want different types of security.

It's crucial that you understand what game you are playing and exactly what you can borrow and when. It's not good, for example, trying to buy a bog-standard 5% rental return buy-to-let terraced house with bridging finance at 15%. The role of bridging finance is to finance tricky, non-standard deals where there is either a large profit margin or where the money is only needed for a short period. It's not intended to finance short-term, low-yielding investments, so you would not use it to purchase a standard buy-to-let.

However, if you had a property you could buy for £90,000, that required a three-month renovation costing £30,000 and afterwards would be worth £180,000, the return would be 50% and the money would only be needed for six months. That's the deal that bridging finance likes to do! After you have had the bridging funds for a few months, you can then re-mortgage onto a standard buy-to-let mortgage which costs 5%.

It's good to look at the cheaper forms of finance first: buy-to-let finance and commercial mortgages tend to be the cheapest, and if they are suitable and can be used then they should be. Also, don't forget that different types of finance can be combined in certain situations. Why would you want to do this? Usually, the answer is to put down as little of your own money as possible into a deal and hence leverage your returns. Banks traditionally have relatively cheap finance but require you to put 30% to 40% into the deal. If you have a limited pot of money, as we all do, then this may mean that you can only do, say, a couple of such deals. But if you can borrow from a private investor and put his money into the deal, it can enable you to do many more deals. Obviously, all parties need to know the structure of the deal and some banks will not want their monies to be mixed with other investors. In fact, most banks are very keen that you put a good amount of money into the deal. They refer to it as having "skin in the game". They are right that from their perspective this is a good thing as it gives you a real added incentive to make sure that the deal is a successful one.

Most investors spend much of their time focusing on the profit margin in a deal, but the sources of finance are equally important and often can be your biggest cost. That's why it's so important to get the right finance and also the most cost-effective one.

POWER PRINCIPLE 16

BUY AND HOLD

Invest for the long term. Despite occasional short-term fluctuations in the UK property market, the long-term trend is up, due to the fundamental reason that demand tends to be greater than supply.

> Real estate is very forgiving over time and, even if you make a mistake by paying too much, the general passage of time will wipe out your mistake.

Real estate is definitely best viewed as a long-term game. Property prices don't increase every year, but over the long term they do. Even though our business plan is to make a lot of money when we have bought and developed a property, we also make a good proportion of our money by the fact that we are landlords and have a rental portfolio that we have built up and kept for the long-term. In fact, it's our business plan never to sell the majority of our portfolio.

It is quite common to make 20% to 40% in a couple of years from buying and developing property and on average only 5% to 10% due to capital appreciation per annum, so why would we choose to keep property? Surely, we would be better focusing on doing developments with their 20% to 40% returns rather than landlording with 5% to 10% returns?

Once you have sold a property, then the gains are immediately taxed and you have to go out and do all the hard work all over again. And developing is hard work.

Holding property long-term is a very tax-efficient thing to do. True, you will not get the big gains from the sales of property, but if you keep it and build a rental portfolio, you get a nice, slow, monthly income stream which over the long-term keeps adding to your bank account and generally at an inflation-linked pace.

It's good to have the two business plans going on hand in hand. Short-term, the developments are a great form of business to be doing. Medium to long-term, holding real estate and landlording is a great business plan.

One point to bear in mind is that although the short-term development profits are better than long-term buy and hold, there is also a lot more work (way more, in fact) involved in doing a development. Developments and renovations are hard work and require as much skill as a professional occupation.

Landlording tends to be easier than developing. I see my developments like my day job (because it is!) and the rental portfolio as more like a savings account.

The compound effect of capital appreciation is a great builder of wealth in the long term.

The fact that the buy and hold strategy is so successful can be evidenced by the fact that a lot of high-net worth individuals hold a lot of their money in property, even though they may not have made it in real estate. In fact, the percentage of high-net-worth individuals owning rental property (both commercial and residential) is sky-high.

Even though the capital appreciation side of things usually results in some very good long-term profits, it can't however be relied upon or predicted in advance. You never know from year to year what will happen to the price of real estate. Each year, economists try and focus on how much real estate will increase by, and every year (usually in January) there are many projections and predictions. There is absolutely no way you should listen to any of these and base any financial plans on them. Prices can go up or down during any given year. Capital appreciation is best viewed as a bonus. It will happen over time but it cannot be quantified, pinpointed or predicted in advance.

By holding real estate long-term, landlords can grow rich in their sleep without working or taking any risks.

POWER PRINCIPLE 17

ONLY SELL IF YOU NEED THE MONEY

Many people ask when you should sell real estate. This is a very good question if you view real estate as a solid, long-term investment, which I do.

Many people have a "never sell" attitude as they like to benefit from capital appreciation. As a general rule, when I decide to buy and keep a property I do not have a pre-determined sales date in mind. Be in real estate for the long-term and if you don't need to sell, don't sell. If you can't put the money to better use, then don't sell. Let your money sit in the property and enjoy the relatively-easy returns of landlording and capital appreciation.

Maybe you are happily getting 5% capital appreciation and a 5% rental return per annum, and have been doing for many years. These are nice, solid and very easy long-term returns, that don't require that much daily hard work from you. Why change such an easy and fairly predictable business plan?

Maybe a deal is placed in your lap that will earn you 30% or 50% return instantly, but you don't have the money available in cash to put into the deal. Then, it may make perfect sense to sell one of your properties to access that money. In that case, you should sell the property and use the money to buy the higher-returning investment. A 30% to 50% return trumps a 10% return, after all.

If you don't have sexy deals like that hitting your plate that you can use the money for, then it's probably best to keep your money in your property and sit back and let it ride out for the long-term play. There are very few people who have lost money on property if they have held it for 10 plus years. This is one of the best aspects of property.

POWER PRINCIPLE 18

DON'T BE A FIRST MOVER BUT ALSO, DON'T FOLLOW THE CROWD

Pick an up-and-coming area, not necessarily an already-established one, but one where there's already good momentum. Many people follow the money and there is a lot of wisdom here. If an area is increasing in popularity, it will have its own self-generating momentum. It's good to jump in, follow the money and be a part of it. It's like riding a wave. If you have the force of a wave behind you, then it's easy to stand up on the board and move forwards. If you don't have the power of the wave, it's pretty tricky to stand up, let alone move forwards.

Once the momentum is there, it is usually safe to assume that it will continue and you can expect above-average growth as more and more people and businesses are attracted to an area.

> The earlier you get in, the riskier the investment strategy – but potentially the reward is the highest.

It's good to get in at the start of the process, as quite often you can buy relatively cheap real estate before demand outstrips supply. Often, this patch sees the biggest percentage price increases. However, investing in an area that is still not gentrified and recognised as a desirable place to live requires some serious due diligence. The biggest and best gains tend to occur right at the start, and that's where the brave money enters the market. It's the stage where things are not certain and you could end up buying in an area that doesn't make it. Risk and reward tend to go hand in hand here.

Quite often, you find that there is a desirable area near or next to a less-desirable area. When prices rise too much in the desirable area, the less-desirable area tends to increase and experience a bit of a ripple effect. When people can no longer afford to live in the desirable area, supply and demand has gotten out of sync somewhat. Some people will be priced out of the area or some people may just think that the less-desirable area is better value. In my chosen areas, the same amount of money would buy a two-bedroom flat in Chorlton or a three-bedroom house in Whalley Range, less than a mile down the road. Some will choose the flat to be in the centre of the action and close to all the amenities. Some will choose a house to have a bigger and better property.

If you see the young trendy types entering an area and the odd coffee shop or internet café cropping up, maybe even a hipster real ale pub, then it's a fairly safe bet that the area is in the process of gentrification and you're probably safe to start looking at deals in that area.

Don't jump in before you see some serious signs of gentrification. You don't need to take unnecessary risks that are outside of your control in real estate. If you get average returns in real estate (and leverage them accordingly), you can do very well and by picking the right up-and-coming area, you can get better-than-average returns and supercharge your profits.

POWER PRINCIPLE 19

REAL ESTATE IS A PEOPLE GAME

Learn negotiation, sales, presentation skills and most importantly become a people person. Real estate is a people game.

As a real estate investor, you will be using a lot of very specific and important skills during your career, covering many different aspects of real estate. You will be involved with everything from the finance, the legals, building works, interior design, planning, risk management. The list goes on. However, one common underlying theme is people skills. It's the foundation on which most of the other specific skills are built.

I deal with and meet thousands of people in my business every year and, without exception, I only have business relationships with people that I like. And I assume they only deal with me because they like me. Of course, we need to know that we can make money together. That's the point of doing business. However, there's a lot of money out there in the world and wouldn't you rather do business with someone you like? I'm not meaning someone who likes the same football club as you, or dresses the same, or who has the same hobbies (although this definitely helps. Any area of mutual interest helps). I'm meaning someone that you can look at deep down and say that you like, trust and respect as an individual. Someone who you would choose to spend time with and who has all the right characteristics that would make you want to partner with them. Someone you would trust to make money for you and your family.

Being liked comes first, and then at a deeper level comes being trustworthy. You can't have trust without shared values.

> **If people like you, they will listen to you, but if they trust you, they'll do business with you.**

Now, I'm not saying that you should always shun people you don't "gel" with. I have done business with many different types of people. In the past, I have done a lot of business with people I don't really like or trust, but in these cases the deal was always a one-off and the returns were potentially very good.

What I would say is that I have never enjoyed a deal and made as much as a profit as I could have done, with people I don't like or trust.

I find that when I deal with people I don't trust, they tend to confirm my suspicions that they are untrustworthy. Quite often they will renegotiate the deal as they go on, very often at the last minute. If you find yourself in a situation where the deal looks good but the person on the other side doesn't, then you need to be 100% on your game.

I normally have a trust-but-verify policy when doing business. This goes out of the window if I'm dealing with someone who I don't trust 100%. Then, your guard needs to be up. You need to question everything that is told to you and also be thinking about what hasn't been told to you. What could they be hiding or planning to do? It takes up a lot of brain time doing this, and although it's good to keep this part of your brain trained every now and again, it's a pretty miserable way to do business and lead your life.

It's far better to find partners who are trustworthy, honest individuals whose word you can rely on and to do business with them. These are the people you end up doing repeat deals with. You can build a relationship of trust and business becomes so much easier then. I have one private investor that I have done many of my deals with and I have always had at least one project on the go with him for the last 14 years. I know his investment criteria and if I need money and the deal is right for him, I will call him up and within a few minutes he's given me an answer. As I know his investment criteria so well, it's usually a "yes." I don't waste his time with deals that would be unsuitable for him and he doesn't waste mine by going through the motions and then not actually funding the deal, as is so common with many want-to-be investors.

We have spent years working with each other and developing trust between us. It's far better to find someone you like and then start building a relationship of mutual trust, than it is just to be chasing one-off deals.

As well as really connecting with partners and people doing the actual deals, there are also a huge amount of people that you will just come across during the course of your business. There will be people doing maintenance on your properties, surveyors, cleaners, mortgage brokers, estate agents, lawyers, builders, landscapers, suppliers, designers. The better the relationship you have with pretty much everyone you meet during the course of your business, the more enjoyable and successful your business will be. It enables things to get done in a quicker, smoother and more efficient way.

It makes you enjoy the process more, and enjoying the process is absolutely key to longevity in business and success generally. By "process" I mean the day-to-day work you do in business. If you don't enjoy your day-to-day work, and view it only as a means to getting rich and making money, then you almost certainly won't realise that goal as you won't be working hard enough. I enjoy my work so much and work with some of the most amazing people, that I would do it even if I wasn't paid.

For some people, good interpersonal skills come naturally. For others, they don't. They didn't really come naturally to me in the early days. I was a lawyer by profession and when I gave this up and started my journey as a property investor, I had to really focus on my interpersonal skills. I was used to being surrounded by other lawyers and suit-wearing businessmen and I felt at home in this environment. I used to spend many, many hours buried in paperwork trying to find the one bit of evidence that would make or break our case. I wasn't necessarily interacting with people as often as I would be when I became a businessman.

When I left my nice, air-conditioned office in London and moved onto a building site in Manchester, I experienced a very dramatic change in the types of people I was dealing with. The diversity of people was far wider for a start. I can be dealing with lawyers, accountants, salesmen, architects, interior designers, builders, carpet suppliers, stone masons, coffee shop owners, website designers, social media experts all within a one-hour time period. And that's without even mentioning property investors themselves (who are very hard to stereotype).

If you are not a naturally personable person, then there are many things you can do to improve yourself in this area. The Internet is full of resources to help you gain these skills. The two I like the best are active listening (ie. listening, rather than talking) and mimicking. With active listening, the aim is that you let the other person dominate and lead the conversation. Your goal is to let them talk, as people generally love talking. This enables you to get a lot of information from them and also creates a good relationship with them as you have allowed them to talk and hopefully shown interest in their topics of conversation. The second skill is mimicking. By mimicking, I mean making yourself more like the person you are dealing with. If they dress in a certain way, you match them. If they like talking about football, you do the same and raise it as a topic of conversation. If they like having a meeting in a café, suggest meeting them in a café. If they always write notes down in a meeting, make sure you take a pad with you and make some notes as well. It helps identify you as part of their tribe and creates a feeling of rapport and safety.

Improving and working on your interpersonal skills is a process. It's a skill to learn. It shouldn't be about putting on some fake front that you're using to try to "con" someone into liking you and doing business with you. That's not going to work, in fact it's just false and wrong. Getting good interpersonal skills is about developing and projecting the best parts of your personality so that you can talk with and interact better with people, rather than sitting there quietly and not having the confidence to address someone. You need to learn how to best interact with people in a way that makes you a pleasure to be around and to do business with. This will make doing business far more enjoyable, not just for the people you are dealing with, but primarily for you.

KNOW YOUR EXIT STRATEGY OR STRATEGIES BEFORE BUYING

It's no use buying a property if you have no plan for it and can't make any money from it. You have to know how you are going to make money from it.

There are many different ways of making money from real estate if you are an investor/developer. Some people will want to buy and sell it quickly. Some will want to rent it. Some will want to do either small or massive amounts of work to it, to realise exponentially more profit, and then either sell or rent it. There are various themes around these areas, and many different business plans, but the main two ways of realising a profit from a property are by selling or renting it.

Both of these strategies are quite different. Selling is final and short-term. When it's sold, it's generally gone and the value of the asset is realised and turned into cash. The cash value is then taxed accordingly.

If it's rented, then the income stream and also the liabilities of the building (maintenance, mortgage etc.), go on for as long as it's owned and rented. Selling is a short-term business plan and renting is a long-term one. Whichever plan you choose, you need to make sure you have done your due diligence and got the strategy right.

There isn't a right or a wrong strategy. Both have their pros and cons. What you need to make sure is that you are going into a deal and operating with your eyes open and that you know what your exit strategy is.

Let's take an example of an investor wanting to set up an HMO to secure a great rental return. This is a very standard business plan for investors, especially in today's market. You buy a big house – four or five bedrooms – change a lounge downstairs into a couple of small bedrooms and, all of a sudden, you have seven rentable rooms bringing in £400 each a month (so £2,800 in total), whereas rented as a single family unit the rental income may only be £1,500. This strategy will turbo-charge your rental returns if you're a landlord. However, once this has been done, you are limiting your exit strategy, which is fine if you know what you are doing. Once set up as an HMO, the only people who will usually buy such a building with its small bedrooms (and quite often, lots of en suites and maybe kitchen facilities in the rooms), will be other investors. That's a small market compared to selling to first-time buyers, families, and/or investors. It's maybe 10% of the overall sales market.

If your goal is to carry on and achieve a rental return, then the HMO strategy is a great long-term one. If you need to exit quickly and sell, it may be more problematic.

Whenever I go into a deal, I always have two exit strategies. I aim at a very wide market when I am both selling and renting. I target affluent millennials or, more usually, millennials with affluent parents! When we buy a property, we always know if it will be a good rental property or a good one to develop and sell. Usually, in our area the property will tick both boxes, as people would ideally love to live here as an owner-occupier, but also people who couldn't afford to buy would love to rent our properties as well. Our area of South Manchester is quite a desirable area. This is not just luck. We chose to invest in our particular area because of this fact, or at least it was a very strong factor in our decision-making process.

I have a general rough-and-ready business plan of keeping 25% of everything we build for the business as rental properties and selling 75%.

It's generally easier to rent than it is to sell, so every development we do when we are selling the flats, I am fully prepared to keep them if any of them don't sell. We can rent them, remortgage them and get our profit out that way, along with our rental income. So far, I have never had to do this as we have sold all the flats we have ever marketed, but as a fall-back plan it's a good one.

Knowing your exit strategy is key. Having a fall-back exit strategy in case the first one does not work out is even better. Having three or four exit strategies ... now we're talking!

POWER PRINCIPLE 21

YOU MAKE YOUR MONEY WHEN YOU BUY, NOT WHEN YOU SELL

When you buy a property you should already know what you are going to do with it and what profit margin there is in the deal. Never buy a piece of real estate when you don't know where the profit is or if you are waiting for the unpredictable nature of capital appreciation to kick in before you can aim to sell it at a profit. Never buy a property thinking that you will beat the averages with capital appreciation. Trying to bet on future capital appreciation is speculation. It is gambling on future events. It is not investing and is certainly not a viable business plan.

You need to be able to clearly see the deal and the profit margin at the precise moment you are buying it. Often, this can be buying a property below market value; usually, it is doing some renovation or development work to the property and so realising the profit through sweat equity.

With residential property, usually it will take a few months (or even a couple of years) on bigger schemes, to realise the profit, but it should be very certain that when you buy a property there will be a clear and achievable route to making the profit. That's why I say: you make your money when you buy, not when you sell. The purchase price you pay will determine how much profit you end up making at the end of the deal.

And remember: when we are talking about making money, we are referring to cold hard cash in the bank. We are not referring to paper profits. It's no good having a great-looking balance sheet if you have no money in the bank or no cash flow coming in. That's how "successful" businesses go bust. I have a general principle that I need to see my profit (or a good chunk of it at least) back out of a deal within two years.

The relatively long-term nature of this is because I do building work that can take up to 18 months or so. If you are just doing single houses, then you're probably best aiming for profit out of a deal in less than a year.

POWER PRINCIPLE 22

THE 18-YEAR PROPERTY CYCLE

Property goes up, plateaus, or goes down in value and you can make money because of this.

You can't tell the precise timing of what will happen to the property market or the extent of what will happen to price falls or rises, but by studying the history of property cycles you can actually get a very good idea of what will come next.

Many economists agree that there are fairly regular seven to eight- or 18-year property cycles. If you look back to World War Two (and some economists actually go back way further than this), then there is some strong evidence that 18-year cycles do tend to repeat, for whatever reason. From an analysis of these cycles we can see common factors. Usually, there is a nice slow and steady uptick in prices and activity from years 0 to 7. There then tends to be a plateau for a few years (between years 7 to 10) while the market catches up with itself. Prices and activity during this patch tend to be slow and often stagnant. Then, years 10 to 15 tend to be a bit more buoyant, with there usually being a year or two of quite high property price appreciation. These are the boom years. These are the years of irrational exuberance. It's not unusual to see years here where you can experience gains of 15% to 20%. Then, as winter follows autumn, so bust follows boom and we see two to three years of price falls (the bust years) until the market has corrected and we are back at the start of the cycle again.

The psychological reasons for these cycles are fairly obvious to explain in general terms. If you are unsure where you are exactly in a current cycle, it's worth speaking to people and finding out how they view real estate. This should give you a good idea of where you are in the cycle and, most importantly, what will be coming next. After all, it is people who buy property (or not) and who cause the prices to go up or down, so people's psychology is key in this process.

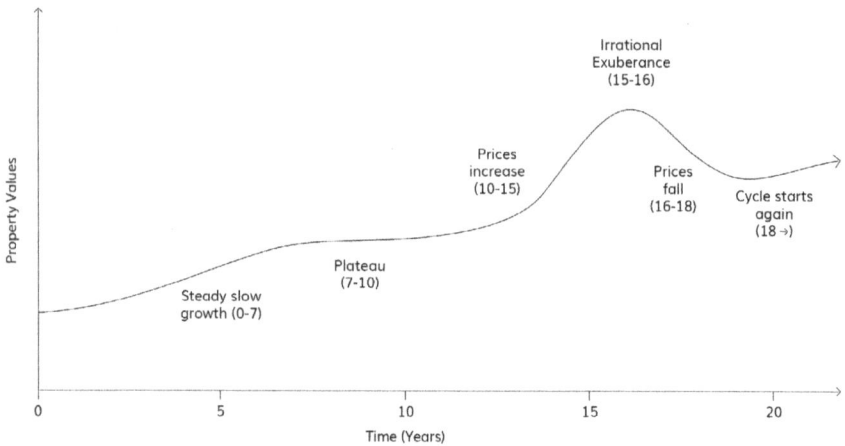

At the first stage, people have just experienced the bust, a few years of property falls, and are dubious about property investment. Property as an asset class is not flavour of the month. There is no rush to get back into the market and everyone is a bit sceptical about how stable the market is. But it's an established asset class and also a place to live, so for the first seven or so years of a cycle, it slowly plods along and increases in value. It's usually always slow at first as the last recession is fresh in people's minds.

After three to five years, people are more comfortable with real estate and prices tend to increase a bit quicker. Values usually increase faster than wages during this stage. Then, like a stretched elastic band, as prices have outpaced people's earning power, people can no longer afford property and the process slows down to reasonable growth levels again. People are usually quite rational about prices during this period and sensible decisions are often made based around the affordability of property. This usually results in a mid-cycle plateau for a period of several years. Prices tend to stagnate, although rarely go down. There is an expression that real estate is "sticky". This is a way of saying that prices do not often fall as people don't like taking a loss and very few people need to sell real estate as it can usually be rented and lived in rather than sold at a loss. Common sense usually characterises this period as the last property bust is relatively fresh in people's minds and no one wants a repeat of that any time soon.

After the mid-cycle pause, the market slowly picks up again. To start with, price increases are sensible and controlled and largely mirror inflation and people's wage increases for a few years. By now however, the last recession and the turmoil that resulted from it, is a distant memory of 10 years or so ago and a whole new generation of investors and buyers has appeared. Real estate seems solid again: "As safe as houses!" It again becomes a desirable asset class. Prices start to increase, more people see it as a good investment and can see the easy money to be made in the property market and prices go up quicker. It becomes a self-fulfilling prophecy. This is the phase of irrational exuberance and is by far the most active phase of the market where every man and his dog want to get in on the game. In fact, it is almost seen as a status symbol with middle-class people to buy property for bragging rights around the dinner table.

Quite often, you can see prices increasing by 20 to 30 percent in a two-year period, while wages (and hence people's general ability to afford real estate) are still plodding up by 2% to 3%. Obviously this is not sustainable and the inevitable happens and the market stops. All the wind is taken out of its sails. It becomes obvious that normal people can't quite afford it any more. Investors have stopped buying (or at least have become very cautious) several years before, and amateur investors dominate the market during this phase. In fact, any professional in the market is usually outbid by amateurs and they tend not to do much business even if they want to.

By now, property has become too expensive. People can't afford to buy homes to live in and the prices being paid are no longer supportable by the rents being charged. Prices stop increasing and when they do they stop dead, like hitting a wall. Unlike the mid-cycle plateau, now things have become so strained that prices have to fall or snap back (just like the strained elastic band) to get back to reasonable sustainable levels. Prices fall and adjust to make up for the overshooting.

These are the general principles and, importantly, the psychology behind property cycles and you need to know where you are in a cycle. Do not jump in with the rest of the herd when there is already a feeding frenzy in the final stages of a cycle or you could get very hurt. However, you are probably in a safe position if a year or two after a crash, you find a deal that stacks up. In fact, a lot of money is often made during or just after the crash when savvy investors are picking up cheap properties. It's the old business principle of buy low and sell high.

> **Fortunes and strong businesses are built in the bust and collected in the bubble.**

Even though I have laid out here my personal timescales for the various periods, these are only very rough and ready timescales and should not be used to guide your investment-making process. "What!" I hear you say. "This is a book about investment and making money not some economist's musings?" And you are right. I'm certainly no economist. You need to roughly know where you are in a cycle, but you can never know for certain and you can never say precisely when markets will turn. If you think you can buy a piece of real estate at the bottom of the cycle and then diarise 18 years later and sell it at the top, you are very mistaken. If you do this, you may miss the biggest growth phase which might happen at 18 to 20 years. Or you might even be selling at the bottom of the market, as the market may have turned at year 16. These are general principles and should be understood, looked at, but not relied on for the details of your business plan.

POWER PRINCIPLE 23

BUY FOR CASH FLOW RATHER THAN CAPITAL APPRECIATION

One of the best entry-level books on real estate investing is *Rich Dad, Poor Dad* by Robert Kiyosaki. It was written in 1997 and its message is basic but timeless. Its general principle is that you should make sure you buy an asset not a liability. According to Kiyosaki, an asset puts money in your pocket each month and a liability takes it away each month. This is a very simplistic but very correct statement. Kiyosaki was, and still is, an amazing real estate investor and his advice is absolutely on point. If I could give one piece of advice to all newbie real estate investors, it would be this one. In fact, his books are absolute must-reads for anyone contemplating a real estate investing career. Buy for income, buy for cash flow.

> **Make sure each property you buy goes on to put surplus money in your pocket each and every month.**

It's simple maths but often investors actually over look this point. "Why?" you may ask? Well, some investors don't need surplus income (or extra income tax!) as they may already have good paying jobs. They may be buying for the long-term capital appreciation. Many high-net-worth employees view property as a great asset class primarily for its tax advantages and buy it for this reason and for capital appreciation. In fact, some investors are quite happy to buy a property that makes a rental loss each month as they are banking on the appreciation. Well, what if they lose their job and they are stuck with a loss-making investment?

My contention as a professional investor is that capital appreciation should be seen as a bonus, not as the main aim of the investment. True, capital appreciation tends to make up a very big chunk of real estate profits, but it's very hard to predict when you will receive it. It's a very safe bet to say that you will have seen significant capital appreciation over a 10-year plus period. But you never know when it's going to happen – and if your cash flow is negative and you are forced to sell, you may well never see any of it. Real estate is one of the best ways to make money but it has to be well-positioned as an asset, not a liability.

Banking on capital appreciation is basically speculation. Setting up a good property, ensuring that it is well-maintained, clean, tidy and meeting your tenants' needs, where the rent exceeds the mortgage payments and other associated payments, that's an investment.

There are plenty of investment properties out there that can be well-positioned assets rather than liabilities, and which also have a strong chance of getting a very good amount of capital appreciation. Buy them and structure them so that they put money into your pocket each and every month, after all expenses have been paid for.

POWER PRINCIPLE 24

YOU NEED TO STAND OUT AND BE OUTSTANDING!

Property is one area of business where you can be average and still make some decent returns. I see average investors and developers every day buying, selling and holding property for the long-term and making a really good profit because of this. In fact, this is the cornerstone of many of the property training courses and companies out there, and rightly so.

You need to learn what works. Learn how buy-to-lets, HMOs, developments, etc., operate and master the basics of these areas. However, once you have learnt the basics and learnt what works and what does not, then if you can improve on your standard to the point that you are better than the crowd, the returns can be exponential.

> The investor who manages to stand out from the crowd finds themselves in a very sweet position: the investors in second and third position get proportionally far less than the best investor.

Have you ever wondered why markets tend to be dominated by one brand and the next best brands are quite far away from the leader? Look at the dominance of Gillette for example. I'm not sure I even know which the second best shaving cream is. The obvious choice is to choose the best; why would anyone choose the second best? So everyone chooses the best and even if it's only slightly the best everyone buys it.

To get these super-charged returns you need to stand out and be better than the competition. There is a lot of property out there and there is a lot of competition amongst the various investors and developers. You need something to give you an edge.

If you want superior returns, don't aim to be one of many average vanilla or magnolia properties around. I refer to bog-standard average or below-average properties as "magnolia properties" as many average investors/developers paint their properties in magnolia (or "Maggie"!) as it's cheap, light and bright and hides a few scuffs here and there. It's become an industry standard for average and boring. We don't use Maggie any more.

A buyer looking to buy a property will buy the best property in their price range. This is a very important point to bear in mind. They won't buy the second or third best. There is only one winner and that winner needs to be you. In short, you need to stand out and differentiate yourself from the competition. You need to be the best. So how do you do this?

You need laser-like focus and hard work. You need to pay attention to the thousands of details that make up your property. You need to make sure that everything you do is amazing and well thought out. You need to be the world's best at what you do.

We aim to be the world's best developers of blocks of renovated flats in South Manchester. It's been hard to get to that position and it's been a long process. It probably took us 10 years or so. However, the whole time we were aiming to get to this position, and we were going from average to market leader, we were still enjoying good returns and we could see that with every job we did, our returns were getting better.

As you become increasingly successful, other developers will try to copy you and take your buyers. They will find out what materials you use and they will start using them. I know, as this has happened to us several times. The competition may get a few of your details, but they won't get all of them, and inevitably they will end up looking ill-thought-out. One developer copied our pattern a few years ago, very successfully. I walked into one of her apartments and it was like one that we had done ... when we were drunk!! It had the right things in there, but it was badly executed. That particular developer had missed 50% of the details that we had worked out and perfected over the years. We upgraded some of our fixtures and fittings after that, and we never saw that developer again.

Don't worry about other developers stealing your design work. Worry about when they stop!

There are no short cuts in this area and there are no rest days. You constantly have to be trying to become the best or, if you are the best, you need to keep improving to keep the position. Always deliver more than expected.

It's a great touch if there is a gimmick or something a bit flamboyant that people notice that makes you stand out. One thing that we have found that works well is to really emphasise the open day. We usually have a lot of publicity for our open houses and have champagne, beer and chocolates on offer. No one else does that in our area and people notice and talk about it. It's nice to have a little buzz like that, something that's eye-catching, but remember that your clients are sophisticated people spending hundreds of thousands on one of your properties. A well-thought-out and modest, eye-catching gimmick may go down well and get you attention, but there is no substitute for doing an amazing job on your development.

Your work has to be amazingly and undeniably good. No Instagram or Facebook campaign can fake that for you or be a substitute for doing an excellent job. Once you have got your amazing product though, then it's good to market and promote it, especially the features that stand out, and create a bit of interest.

POWER PRINCIPLE 25

WORK ON YOUR BUSINESS NOT IN IT

The best role for you in your business is one of strategy, vision and leadership. Everything else is best served by experts who can allow you to focus on the high-revenue-generating tasks. Do not try to be a one-man band doing everything. Instead, you should see yourself as the leader of your business. You are not even a manager. You are a leader.

You need to take control of your business. You are the captain of the ship. You're not the lawyer, the accountant, the builder, the sales or lettings agent, the negotiator. If you want a successful scalable business you need to collect and direct all of your team members. You need a plan and a vision of the business. You need to know where you want to be in one, three, five, 10 and 20 years' time. You are the only person who can achieve that.

The other professionals and experts can do their job. It's your job to make sure they do their job well, but the most important role for you is one of strategy and leadership and you are the only person who can do this job. If you're busy telling the handyman what handles to use on a kitchen cabinet (which is a job that has to be done right, after all) then you are missing the opportunity of spending time focusing on the biggest, heaviest-hitting aspects of your business.

You need to have a plan of where you are going. If you don't know where you are going, then how do you get there? You need a very clear vision of where you are, where you want to be and which road you need to travel down to get there. You need to work out the obstacles and the challenges, work out your business plan and assess if it's a price worth paying to get there.

In 2006, I decided I wanted to be the best developer in one postcode in South Manchester, specialising in high-end apartment blocks. I knew this would be financially very profitable, but it was really the idea and the passion which motivated me. The money follows the passion. I knew this would be hard work. It would involve getting a great architect and getting a lot more property which we could develop and practise on. We already had the foundations of a good business in place, with some great builders and my wife as an amazing interior designer, but we were a long way away from being the best. The goal was to be great, not just good enough.

I saw that there was a market for high-end apartments in our area and that to dominate this area we had to really focus on design (both externally and internally) and build with quality products and materials. Now, I didn't want to (and wasn't able to) throw unlimited money at the situation to achieve this goal. I wasn't about to get Norman Foster or Frank Gehry designing my 10,000 sq.ft. apartment blocks! I needed to make sure that every pound spent generated £1.20 in return.

We started off by slowly but surely making incremental changes to our buildings: a nicer flooring, a better kitchen, a better bath or kitchen tap. Slowly but surely, we started experimenting and adding more quality and design to our jobs. We didn't suddenly jump in with one particular job and totally redesign what we were doing. By going through this process we could then see, in a controlled way, what worked and what didn't.

Fast forward 10 years and we won the UK Property Awards for Best Renovation in the North West 2017/18. With this one moment of recognition, we had achieved our plan. It was a long and difficult road, but the journey was exciting and fun and the destination was everything that I hoped it would be.

We had also managed to raise the ceiling on apartment prices in our area which in itself shows that people were prepared to pay more for our flats than anyone else's.

Although there are many people who can work in your business, there is only one person who can work on your business. There is only one person who can set the tone of the business; one person who can make strategic decisions. If you are not doing this then no one is, and you don't have a sustainable business, you just have a bunch of deals that you have done and when you stop doing deals your business will stop too.

POWER PRINCIPLE 26

ALWAYS LOOK AT WAYS TO ADD VALUE TO YOUR PORTFOLIO

You should be constantly looking at what you already own and which of your properties you can add more value to. Always review what you already have. It's one of the easiest ways to increase your wealth although you may well have to think outside the box here. If you have been used to, and are comfortable with, a property performing in a certain way (and it's a way that works well), it may be hard for you to contemplate doing things differently. If you have a large house that you have been running as a 10-bed HMO for many years, which is very cash flow positive and set up on a very efficient operating system, it may seem counter-intuitive to start looking at ways to change it. Why mess up a perfectly good system? Well, if that same HMO could be split into five flats, which would give you a capital profit margin of an extra £200,000 to £300,000, I would suggest that it would be a move worth considering!

Planning laws change. See if there's any way you can squeeze more value out of what you already own. Council policy is constantly changing and one day, where they have previously been refusing to allow building, they may suddenly change policy and be more in favour of it. In recent years, for example, Manchester City Council has started encouraging developers to build on certain types of plots of land that previously would not have received planning permission. And the uplift from a planning gain is often the biggest profit margin we make in a deal. This is especially true if you already own the property. If you are suddenly in a position where you can stick an extra house in the back of a garden due to a change in council policy, it's basically money for nothing.

When we noticed a change in the council's planning policy, we reviewed all of the properties we owned and found one that had a really large car park and back garden that wasn't really being used that much. We had owned this building for 18 years and when we first purchased it, we approached the council to see if we could build anything in the back. It was quite a firm "no" from them then. However, when we approached them again last year they were more encouraging and, after submitting an application and discussing it with them, we received permission to build an extension with three more two-bed apartments.

Maybe it's just a case of doing a general refresh of your property though. Maybe a lick of paint and new carpet will work out as money well spent. It may be that you focus on the operations side of the property. Is it on the best utilities tariff? Review these. Are you paying an agent too much? Could you self-manage or are you at the scale where it would be more profitable to employ a letting agent full-time in your business? Are all of the expenses that you are incurring necessary?

One of the best improvements we have done on the operations side is to both self-manage our properties and also to employ our own maintenance team. We started self-managing within about five years of starting out and immediately reduced costs by 50%. We were at that time paying a lettings agent about £60,000 per annum in lettings fees. The costs of a full-time agent and marketing fees back then was about £30,000.

The same principle applied to our maintenance as well. When we started paying over £50,000 per annum in maintenance charges to an outside company, we decided it was better to employ a full-time handyman on about half that amount.

Constantly review whether you are missing a trick somewhere. Times change. Business plans should change too. Don't just get caught in your comfort zone. Think outside the box. If you have a particularly old-school attitude to business it may be hard to change your business plan and you may be missing a trick. It's crucial to keep fresh: network with younger investors, see what other business plans are popular, whether they are for you and adapt to changing times. Maybe even employ some people younger than you with a different mindset to you.

POWER PRINCIPLE 27

GO WHERE THE MONEY IS

If you are choosing to do business with someone, would you prefer to be doing business with someone with lots of money or with not much money? There are great returns to be made by focusing on doing business with people who have money. Buy where the wealthy are or where the wealthy are investing. Don't aim to go to the low end of the market. There's not much money there, or if there is, it's very hard to get it.

I have researched many, many types of properties over the years. One type that looks good on paper are properties in low income areas. They are cheap and they can be rented out for good yields. There are plenty of these types of properties available, especially in the North of England, in and around the main cities. The yields look amazing and it would be easy on paper to see how you can very quickly build up a large portfolio of highly cash-flow-positive properties. This can be a profitable business plan and some landlords do it very successfully.

However, there are many downsides to this type of business plan and it tends to be hard work dealing with people who can only afford to live in cheap properties. You are, in effect, asking them for (rental) money when they don't have much money.

I find it's better to target a market where there is already money. Go where the money is and you have a better chance of making some. If there's no or little money in an area, you're not going to make much.

Not only is it relatively easy to deal with and do business with people who have money but they also tend to have a positive effect on the area and, by association, on the house prices. If an affluent person buys a house in an area and, after a few years, it starts to need a lick of paint or a nice new fence, then the owner has the money to do this. They have surplus money to keep their properties looking nice. Other buyers are attracted by this. They see nice houses and want to live there too. It gentrifies an area and, very importantly, creates demand. When there is demand there is upward pressure on prices, and that is what all investors are looking for at the end of the day.

The infamous American bank robber, Willie Sutton, was once asked why he robbed banks and he replied, "Because that's where the money is!" I would recommend investing in more affluent areas rather than poorer areas, and in more expensive rather than lower-end properties, for the very same reason.

POWER PRINCIPLE 28

HAVE INTEGRITY AND
DO WHAT YOU SAY

People buy and sell to people who they like and trust. Now, this may sound very obvious and not worth stating, but it's a key concept on a couple of different levels.

There is the basic honesty level (you need to be a moral and honest person), but going deeper than this (and especially due to the advent of social media) you are now your own personal brand.

You need to act with integrity and you need to embody the image and idea of who you are.

In real estate, your word is your bond.

The real estate world is actually quite a small world. I know pretty much everyone operating on the ground in my area. I also know a lot of investors (through networking, conferences, seminars, etc.), who operate in the same field as me but in different geographical locations. Most of these people are normal, honest and trustworthy people. Every now and again, an investor or someone in the industry does something unethical. Someone lies about a deal or breaks their word in some way. News of this travels fast and that person is basically dead in the water.

Social media enhances this. It's very common on the forums and WhatsApp groups that I am on for investors to ask questions about new people they are thinking of dealing with. "Has anyone done business with Mr X?" or "Can anyone recommend a good architect?" etc., are almost daily questions I see. Just one or two replies can have a serious effect both positively and negatively on you.

In the age of social media, it is especially important to have integrity and to do what you say. Actually, you always have been your own personal brand but now it is out there on social media for the whole world to see with the click of a mouse. Twenty years ago, you could hide in the shadows. Now, this is becoming increasingly difficult and we all have a social media presence, even if we don't know it.

There is a lot of business that is done in real estate without legal contracts being signed or without much legal protection being afforded, so it's vital that you are able to trust what people say and what they say they will do. If you can't trust someone's word, then there's a lot of wasted time and wasted opportunities, and potentially lost money. It's very hard to do a good deal with a bad person and if someone starts being less than honest with you, you should walk away very quickly.

POWER PRINCIPLE 29

YOUR PERSONAL REPUTATION IS YOUR BRAND

Your personal reputation is the foundation of your business and everything is built upon it. You differentiate yourself from the competition by your personal brand and this stems from your integrity. A personal brand isn't something you can outsource. By its very definition, this is 100% you and how you behave.

There are lots of deals out there, so you never need to be greedy with one particular deal. You can't go broke taking a profit, even if it's a small one.

> **You can't go broke taking a profit.**

There are 25 million homes in the UK. There are a lot of potential deals that can be done. At any one time, we always have several sales and purchases that we are doing and dozens of potential deals that we are looking at, doing our due diligence on and/or negotiating. Finding deals is not usually a problem. The problem is time. There are more deals out there than you can possibly manage.

When you realise this, it's a very liberating feeling. You can go to your networking events or talk to other investors online with a bit of a sense of security. Never be afraid to talk to another investor about what you are doing, where and how. I do this all the time. Now, in theory, the other investor could come and compete against us. He could do what

I'm doing, do it better and take all my business. In practice, that's never happened. It's never got close to happening and it never will. There are just too many deals to go around.

Do not fall victim to "deal fever." Deal fever is a phenomenon that occurs when you see a deal and you have to have it. You really just have to have it. The reasons aren't important: what is important is that logic seems to go out of the window. You experience emotions more akin to people who go shopping on a weekend for clothes they don't really want or need, to gamblers or alcoholics and/or druggies. It sounds a bit dramatic but I've seen investors get so caught up and excited by deals that these analogies are true ones.

You start massaging the figures to make the deal stack up. The costs come down on your spreadsheet, the sales prices go up and the next thing you know you have a deal that stacks and you are pursuing it. The chase is on! There may be other investors after the property, but you are going flat out to get it. Victory will be yours!

This is fine if it's a true deal. Just make sure that it is. Stop, breath and then go back to basics ... look at the financials. Then look at the financials again. If it's not as good as you'd like it to be, walk away. It may be hard. You will lose the prize, but sometimes the prize isn't worth it.

> **Win-win outcomes may be difficult to create, but they are always the best ones.**

Don't be greedy in a deal. There is usually plenty of money to go round. If you intend to create relationships with people that last for many deals and many years, you need to make the process an enjoyable one and you need to be fair not greedy. Always make sure everyone in the deal is happy and is making a profit. If necessary, leave some money on the table. Don't necessarily negotiate as hard as you can if it will sour relationships.

If you are doing a deal and there is not as much profit in it as you would have liked, don't be bitter. Take a small profit and move on. You will never go bust taking a profit.

POWER PRINCIPLE 30

YOUR STAFF ARE YOUR BEST ASSETS

Hire great staff. Hire the best people you can possibly find, people who are better than you, and then treat them really well. Your staff are your best assets and any scalable business will be built on them. You want to find staff that you like and trust. You are going to be spending most of your waking day with your staff, so make sure that you really like and respect the people you have hired.

It's actually really cost-effective to hire the best, even if this means spending more on their salaries. I used to think it was good business practice to find cheap staff and cheap tradesmen. Actually, this thought process back-fired many, many times and the old cliche that, "if you pay peanuts, you get monkeys" is really true.

It's far better to focus on finding an amazing employee and then paying what it takes to employ them or keep them. I would never settle for a member of staff who was just average or somewhere around average. I would always look to employ someone who was outstanding and amazing at their job.

In fact, you want to get to the position where your staff are so passionate and so good at their job that they treat the business as if it were their own.

We have already discussed that you should find the best professionals you can. This is important as the deals you will be doing will eventually be high value and, if handled well, there will be some potentially great profits to be made. Choosing great talent is even more important when you are establishing your team and employing permanent members of staff. It's imperative that you pick the best. This really cannot be overstated. These are the people that will be running a part of your business for you after all.

> **If you take care of your employees, then your employees will take care of your business.**

Real estate is a big money game and the cost difference between hiring and paying for the best, compared to paying for average or second-rate staff, is minimal compared to the figures and profit margins available. A lot of employees in the property game will be working on deals that are worth 100 or 200 times their annual salary. Just a few percentage increase in their performance would be paid for many times over. It's always worth it to employ high achievers who cost you more in salary, yet who will make you far more in income.

As well as looking at the staff individually when you are recruiting, you also need to think about how they will gel and function as a team. It's hard to engineer in advance, but when you are recruiting have one eye firmly on what the team will look like as a whole. You need the right people and the right chemistry. I have personally used the Wealth Dynamics personality test created by Roger Hamilton. His website has a test which is a series of questions (only about 30 of them) that give you a work profile of your personality. It's uncanny how accurate it is after only 30 questions and I highly recommend you use it on yourself and potential staff members. By testing potential staff in advance, I can see what areas they are suited to and it's a great resource for making sure that I am not making a mistake by hiring them for one job when they should really be doing a different job.

As property is quite a high value, high-profit industry; you can make a good return without having too many staff. Many studies say that six is a good number of staff to have in a team. I agree. Six people can do a lot and more than that tends to become a bit unwieldy.

Jeff Bezos, the entrepreneur founder of Amazon, once said that if you can't feed a team with two pizzas then it's probably too big. I prefer to say that if you can't sit everyone comfortably round a pub or restaurant table and talk to everyone easily, your team is probably too big.

When you have assembled your team, you need to make sure you treat them very well. You are the leader of the team and you need to take this role seriously and really focus on providing them with everything they need to do an amazing job. You need to make sure they are happy, well paid and fulfilled with the quality of their work.

I find that employees generally have three prime needs. They need interesting work. They need acknowledgement and recognition for doing a good job. They need to be kept informed of what is going on in the company they work for, and they need to feel like they own or part-own it. Appreciate everything your staff do. Nothing else can take the place of a few well-chosen, sincere words of praise. They're free to give out and the return on Investment is worth a fortune.

Try to avoid the temptation to micromanage your staff. You should give them responsibility to do their job without detailed interference from you. Yes, you are an entrepreneur and, by nature, want to be in control. You have probably left a company job and employer and gone out on your own to start a business. You want control, but you have to resist the urge to micromanage. Nothing will kill staff motivation, and hence their performance, quicker.

There is a time and a place for micro-managing and it's not when it comes to dealing with staff. It's in the planning and design stage of your work, when you are working out your build and are looking at the details of the properties you will be building. Then, it's absolutely encouraged to be a micro-manager. At this stage, I am heavily involved with the details and I am always discussing them with the builders, architects and designers.

And remember, today with millennials and the Internet, the business environment is not what it was 20 years ago. Today, no one works for you. That's right, they don't work for you, they work for themselves – and if working for you is not in their best interests, they will not slog it out for another 20 years like their parents did. They probably won't even slog it out until the end of the month. If they are not feeling valued and satisfied, they will pack up and leave you in a heartbeat. Today, no one works for you or for a boss any more. Everyone works for themselves. However, if they are being financially and emotionally-rewarded, they will go the extra mile for you.

POWER PRINCIPLE 31

CASH RESERVES BEAT CASH FLOW

You should always have a substantial cash buffer. The investors who get into difficulty are often the ones who do not have any spare cash to access in case of an emergency. As an investor, you will incur unexpected costs and you should have some spare cash to cover these situations. The size of this buffer depends on your personal level of risk.

Many investors consider the Holy Grail of property investment to be buying a below-market-value property which cash-flows positive and puts money in their pocket every month. And this is sound as a business plan. There is, however, a twist. I believe that it is actually better to have cash reserves in the bank rather than extra positive cash flow from your property. Cash is king not cash flow. Let's consider an example from a typical BTL property. Say you own a nice, terraced property, single-let, which is 50% geared. Its market value is £150,000; the mortgage is £75,000 which works out at £310 pcm in mortgage payments. The rent is £700 pcm (a 6% yield). This looks great, and it is. There is a surplus of £390 pcm, less expenses, which probably works out at £300pcm profit. This is a solid investment and for many investors this will be an amazing asset to have.

As this property has only a 50% mortgage, you have a financial choice. You can leave it as is and enjoy the lovely positive cash flow or you can remortgage it (leverage up), taking some money out and putting it in the bank. If you remortgage up to 85%, your mortgage goes up to £127,500 and repayments increase to £530. After expenses, you will be lucky to get £100 pcm of positive cash flow. Things are looking a bit tight on a monthly cash flow. However, you have just banked £52,500 from the remortgage.

Now, if you have a maintenance problem how do these two scenarios pan out? If it's a simple one, then it may be payable from the surplus cash flow. Usually, however, it is safe to expect unexpected and high-cost maintenance to occur, and probably when you least want it to. Let's say a boiler fails and needs replacing: that's a bill of over £1,000, instantly, which won't be covered by monthly positive cash flow. It's very, very easy to see situations where even a very conservative and well set up cash flow positive property can get into trouble and incur costs it can't meet. If you have a decent-sized cash reserve in the bank, then any unknown unknowns that crop up can be met and you should never encounter a situation where you can't cope financially.

Having a decent-sized pot of cash will also enable you to potentially do deals which you would not otherwise be able to do and potentially to grow your portfolio more quickly, which in turn will add to your cash flow.

Also, looking at the tax side of things, all rental income is taxable but the remortgage monies are not. Yes, you will be allowing a good pot of money to sit there earning low interest rates (1% to 2% currently in 2019), which you have just remortgaged out at around about 6%. It doesn't make great financial sense if you look at it this way, but this is best viewed as the price you pay for the added security and the potential opportunity value, that a large amount of cash on deposit gives you.

So what is a decent-sized cash reserve to keep? I would aim for at least 10% of a property's value.

Of course, you don't have to choose between cash in the bank and positive cash-flowing properties. In a perfect world, you would have both. However, given a choice (and especially when you are starting your investment career) cash reserves beat cash flow.

POWER PRINCIPLE 32

DON'T LET POTENTIAL PROBLEMS HOLD YOU BACK

Far too often, I have fallen into the trap of worrying about potential problems. Most of these problems never actually happened and I wasted a lot of energy involved in negative conversations with myself.

Imaginary problems often seem too hard to deal with, but the reality is that real problems that are right in front of you can be solved. Make a conscious decision to choose to focus on the problems you have now, not ones that might or might not come to pass in the next one, five, or 10 years' time.

Of course it's good to plan and do your risk management. Don't just blindly charge into a deal without covering all your bases. There is no substitute for risk analysis. Expect good outcomes to happen, but prepare for the worst. However, when you have identified problem areas don't necessarily let these put you off – unless you are very sure they will happen or have a very high likelihood of doing so and if they did happen, they would negatively impact your deal/business to an unacceptable degree.

There is a big difference between worrying, which is self-destructive and negative, and risk analysis. Analyse and identify your problems but don't dwell and focus on them. Focus on and give your time and energy to the solutions.

Even if problems do happen and you have correctly forecast that they do happen, will they really mean that it's the end of your business, the end of the world? More likely, they will just be a negative that has to be dealt with and managed. Apparently, on average at any one point during the day there is someone stealing/shoplifting from a Walmart store. If Sam Walton, the founder of Walmart, was focused on this problem and how to prevent it, he probably wouldn't have managed to turn Walmart into the biggest supermarket chain in the world. He was more focused on how to build and grow his empire. He focused on the positives: the things that made money.

POWER PRINCIPLE 33

DON'T OVERSELL

Sales skills are amazing skills to have and are vital to the success of your business. They should be regarded as one of the foundations of a well-rounded businessman or businesswoman.

You need to spend time learning sales skills. There are lots of books and courses out there and you need to spend as much time as you can educating yourself in this area.

One of the best sales tips I have been given, by an elderly Japanese realtor, Ike, in Canada, is to never oversell. He would present all of the positive arguments for buying a piece of property and then he would stop talking, be quiet and respectfully allow the client to consider them. This enabled him to come across as well-informed and educated about a property but not desperate to close a sale. He would stress the important benefits and selling features of the property but he wouldn't bang on and on about any one topic.

The first time I bought a property from this realtor, I was a lawyer in the UK on a holiday in Whistler, British Columbia. I'd been in Whistler for about 48 hours and had already been blown away by the beauty of the place, so I decided to have a quick look at the real estate market there. He had picked me up and driven me to an apartment that was for sale. He pulled up outside the property and turned the engine off. Before he let me get out however, he handed me a sheet that was entitled, *"Ike's Tips for the Foreign Investor."* It was only a page long and was also in bullet points. There were 10 points in total. He went through them one by one telling me why Whistler was a great area to invest in. Some of these points I knew, but most I didn't. I didn't know, for example, that back then Whistler was preparing a bid to host the Winter Olympics, (a fact that eventually turbo-charged my investment returns). Once he had addressed all of the points, he then went on to tell me why apartments – and especially this apartment – were a good investment. The whole chat lasted only three or four minutes, but by the time I was getting out of the car I was already excited at what I knew was a great investment opportunity. It never felt like a hard sell because it wasn't. It felt like he was working for me and was doing me a great service.

Selling skills are especially important in a culture like the UK where we are traditionally quite reserved. There's nothing more off-putting than a pushy salesperson trying to dominate the conversation and talk you into something. In fact, this usually has the opposite effect and often alienates people, making it hard for the salesperson to close the deal.

Often, once a sale has been agreed it can fall apart due to some element of overselling by too enthusiastic an agent. Don't let this happen to you. If you start talking too much, overselling and promising the buyer too much, even if he doesn't need it, it may well trigger apprehension in the buyer. You may be creating an element of doubt that wasn't even there in the first place, and if a buyer isn't totally convinced in a real estate deal then that deal will not happen.

It's best to concentrate on being personable and building a rapport with your clients, while always accentuating the positive, as opposed to trying to push them into a deal. Be respectful, be honest and be specific in what you claim or say.

> If you are trying to sell, when you've said your bit, stop and be quiet. Don't oversell or you could end up with no sale at all.

If you think you are talking too much and overselling then you almost certainly are. In that situation, stop talking and let the other side say something. Less is sometimes more.

POWER PRINCIPLE 34

FOCUS ON MARKETING
YOUR PROPERTY

You, in close conjunction with your estate agent, will need to market your property very well. This is such an important job that you can't just delegate it to the agent and hope they will take care of it. You need to take a very active and hands-on role here. Of course, a good agent will have their own way of marketing it and you should listen to them and take advice from them. You need to let them do their job. Why have a dog and bark yourself? However, you will also need to put your own brain to work and make sure that, firstly, you have a marketing plan and also that your marketing plan is a great one.

One of the biggest marketing tools you have is your brand. By the time you are starting to think about selling a property you should hopefully already have a brand up and running. Being known locally is great, but in the age of social media it is absolutely essential that you start building up an online brand. You need to put yourself out there on Facebook, Instagram, Twitter, Pinterest, etc.

If it makes you uncomfortable, either suck it up or get someone else to do it for you. There are many agencies and individuals out there who will offer you a social media service. There are some that specialise in UK property and you can either do a quick online search or ask fellow investors for their recommendations. Facebook has lots of property-related groups you can join and these groups are a great source of referrals.

If you can do it yourself though, I would definitely recommend doing so. You yourself are the best person to create your own personal brand. I find it just comes across better when you are being honest and open, rather than employing an agent. When handled well, social media is an amazing business tool for you – and it's pretty much free.

We usually start discussing marketing (both internally and with our agents) as soon as the builders start doing the renovations. There are always going to be some builders to deal with as you would never dream of selling a property without first giving it at least a quick lick of paint, right?!! Work out when the job will be finished and what time of year this will be.

We always have an initial marketing meeting with our chosen agents and this can be up to a year before the job is finished and ready to sell. At this meeting, we will discuss all the measures the agent suggests we use to market the property and we will take advice from them as to what we should be doing.

On our larger blocks, we usually have a hoarding or large boards outside advertising the release date. It's good to create a bit of a buzz around a site and to get potential buyers interested.

Sometimes, we will enter a property for an award that is judged just before the launch date. If we win an award like that, it is marketing gold. If we can stick a board outside a property just as we are releasing the apartments saying that they have won a prestigious award, how do you think that looks to a potential buyer? It looks amazing and is one of the biggest and best things you can do to market your property. Of course, not every development can win an award, although it's actually easier than it looks. Enter a couple of awards just to get a feel for the process and see what happens. You may surprise yourself.

Boards on the outside of the property are key to selling your property. This markets to local people and passing buyers. The Internet is obviously another huge area and you need to make sure your property is on several of the big websites. If your property isn't on Rightmove, then it's basically not for sale as this is where 70% of leads come from. Any good agent will have both boards and internet marketing covered.

We often do open houses. I find they are a good use of time and they create a good sense of urgency and demand. It's great to get a dozen viewers in the same property at the same time. This leads to a sense of competition and urgency and wonderful things tend to happen!

You don't need to employ a professional PR firm but you do need to approach this whole area in a professional and very proactive way. You need to work hard on your marketing, promoting both yourself and also your properties. The two areas are massively interconnected. Marketing is a constant job for a developer but it becomes especially important when a property is being sold.

POWER PRINCIPLE 35

GET A MENTOR OR COACH

If you want to learn, the fastest and easiest ways are to read a book or go on a course. However, in business, academic knowledge only goes so far. One of the best, and fastest, ways to improve your business skills is to spend time and associate with people who are already where you want to be. This can dramatically reduce your learning curve. You can stand on the shoulders of giants. Experience is a great teacher so why not use other people's experiences to supercharge your learning curve?

Get a mentor, a coach, someone whose business plan you admire, someone who is smarter than you, someone who is where you want to be in five or 10 years' time. Spend time with them. Learn from them. Study their habits, how they live their lives and conduct their business. Work out what they do, how they do it, how they think, what makes them tick.

Now, a good professional mentor or coach will cost you money but usually this is one of the best forms of investment you can make. It can be responsible for you doing more deals or deals in better ways and £1 spent on coaching could easily amount to £10 in extra profits.

You want to get as much specific detailed knowledge as you can from them, but there is also so much more you can gain from them. You can get specific property-focused knowledge from books and the Internet. The value in getting a mentor or coach lies in the ability to study, work out and mimic how people you aspire to be like, behave. How do they do business? How do they treat people? What language do they use? What are their daily habits? Where do they spend their time and what do they spend it doing? How do they view business deals? How do they operate? How do they structure their business and their business dealings? If it works for them, and you can see that they have had success through it, then it can work for you as well. That is the true value of getting a mentor or coach.

Surround yourself with people who are on your wavelength and ideally at a more advanced stage along their investment/development journey than you are. They have no doubt spent years learning the hard way. If you can save yourself a few years by learning from their journey and mistakes, why wouldn't you?

I personally have had several mentors/friends who have coached me over the years. Some have mentored me for money, some have mentored me out of friendship and kindness.

Two of the most important and time-consuming areas of my life are property development as a job and, as a hobby, ultra-running. I have coaches for both of these areas and what they give me is priceless.

A coach/mentor will be your voice of reason. They will be the adult in the room. When you are feeling lost or overwhelmed, they should be there for you to guide you through the tough times. They are especially valuable if you are feeling a bit stagnant. You may have a decent business plan and life is generally quite good, but you can't quite see how to take it to the next level. A good business coach can help you break through to the next level.

Challenges, problems, economic uncertainties: the coach will probably have seen it all before and should have the answers. The right coach will be able to analyse your situation and point you in the direction that's best for you and your business.

As well as having been mentored in the past, I have also mentored people ... and I love doing it. It's really great fun and rewarding. You will find that if you ask someone to spend a bit of time with you, talk business and give you a few pointers, they will probably be very keen to. After all, most businessmen like talking business!

POWER PRINCIPLE 36

COMPLETE BEFORE HOLIDAY PERIODS

There is a danger period for deals collapsing and that is during holiday periods (Easter, summer and Christmas ... especially Christmas). I find that deals often fall through during these holiday periods. There tends to be a very familiar pattern. The buyer goes away on a break and meets their friends or family and they manage to sow seeds of doubt in their mind and eventually talk them out of the deal.

It's happened so many times now that this is something I will always focus on when I am doing a deal that may well be drifting over a holiday period. I will try my hardest to get that deal done, or at least exchanged on, before people go off on their holidays.

It may seem a small and trivial point, but deals stretching over holiday periods have been responsible for many failed deals for me. If you have prior knowledge of this, it gives you a tactical advantage.

POWER PRINCIPLE 37

CREATE A SENSE OF URGENCY ABOUT YOUR DEVELOPMENT

One of the best sales tips I have been given is to create a sense of urgency about your property. Now, a good estate agent will be able to do this in a way in which I cannot. They will be able to create FOMO (Fear of Missing Out) and a sense of urgency with the buyer which gives them a push to quickly commit to a property. This ability to create a sense of urgency in buyers is key to getting properties sold quickly. You want them to be chomping at the bit to do a deal. You want them to be overjoyed when you have agreed to sell to them.

A great example of this is Black Friday. People get themselves into a buying frenzy over this weekend. We have all seen the video clips and photos of shoppers queuing for hours to be the first to get into stores and the fights that have broken out over discounted televisions and the like. Shopkeepers and marketers have done an amazing job of turning this weekend into a cash cow by creating a sense of limited time (the sale is for 48 hours only) and hence urgency.

My favourite way of creating a sense of urgency when showing apartments is through open houses or back-to-back viewings, with potential buyers coming in one after another. This not only maximises your time, it creates a sense of urgency and inflated demand.

We will often make a bit of an event of it. We will put on some champagne, beer and nice chocolates just to create a bit of fun and exclusivity. We usually pick a two- to three-hour window for people to view. As our target market is affluent millennials, we usually start at 11am on a Saturday morning and finish at 2pm. When we started earlier, we found that no one came until after 11am. Our high-end starter homes appeal to people that have no kids and like to occasionally go socialising on a Friday night!

We usually get 20 to 30 viewers through the door on the first open house. Half will be timewasters – people who have either made a mistake in coming to view your property or who have a reason other than buying your property, for coming to the viewing. Quite often, other investors will come and have a look at your work for ideas. Sometimes people are just curious and want to see what your property looks like. This leaves about 15 potentials. As we only usually have between eight and 20 units for sale, this can create the impression of a limited supply and often leads to a bit of a frenzy.

POWER PRINCIPLE 38

THE POWER OF VISUALISATION

You need to have a vision clearly focused in your mind when you enter into a deal. You need to know what you want and how it's going to happen. Why do you want to buy this price of property and not another? What are you going to do with it? How will this property make you money?

I generally live in the future. I am usually looking forwards with excitement to what I can do and achieve. Every now and again I come across a person who talks in terms of the past – "the good old days" – and it really clashes with my thought process. I don't look down on those people as I love a bit of history, but it's almost like they are talking a different language. I do not share their sense of comfort with the past. Great things are only achieved by continually looking forwards and projecting into the future. If you stick to what has worked in the past and what was great in the past, then you will either get left behind or you will just continue doing the "same old, same old" stuff and you will in effect just stop growing. Let go of the past and focus firmly on the future. That is the way to grow.

The most exciting times in a transaction for me are when I buy a property, and then less so, when I sell or refinance it, when my vision for that property is accomplished.

I am a very visual person. I see things in my head very clearly and by this, I mean actual pictures of what I want to happen, and things I want to happen that haven't happened yet. These visions are one potential future, one potential outcome that I can achieve and realise if I so desire. I see things that will also enable me to achieve goals. This is not some weird thought pattern. This is a conscious and self-taught strategy. It is a technique called visualisation and is one that I have used in both my business and my sporting life for many years.

When I'm training for 100-mile ultra-marathon races I always think about the race many months in advance using this process. When I'm doing my many long training runs, I can see myself running the race I'm training for. I can feel the terrain, smell the dirt, see the other runners. I go fast up hills if I'm being chased, and always I end up in a sprint finish at some point during my training run! It's almost like I'm a kid pretending, but this is seriously effective stuff and has enabled me to win races.

The last race I ran and won was a 50k race in the Canadian Coastal mountains. Now, my running coach, Gary, is one of the best runners in the world. He was actually hundreds of miles away at the time, but due to the power of visualisation I imagined he was waiting for me about two hours from the finish line, ready to run with me. And he did run with me for the last two hours of the race. He talked to me, he overtook me, he gave me encouragement. He was full of excitement and passion. And how do you think I ran? Below average, average, or like an elite professional ultra-runner? Yes, that's right, I had the run of my life by visualising that he was there beside me!

The same is true for me in business. When I look at a property, I can see what I want to do with it, what needs to happen, which people will help me achieve my goal. I will visualise the end result: a sexy, well-developed, well-designed property with the new owners already living in it, having a nice glass of Rioja after a hard day in the office. And this all happens before I have purchased it.

From the moment I first see a property, I can usually see two years into the future to when the job is finished. I know who the builders will be and how many apartments we will be able to fit into the property. I visualise what the building has the potential to be. I will visualise what it looks like both internally and externally. I will visualise the clean brick, and a smart extension at the back of the building. I will know in advance what materials we will be using and where the living areas will be situated to make best use of the sunny aspects. I will even visualise where the car park will be, what materials it will be built with, and what type of cars the end buyers will have parked there.

I have a goal for that property, a vision of what we can make it, and I know the business plan that will achieve the goal. This is what being a property developer is all about for me. It's the realisation of a goal. It's a clear vision of what you want to do both for your business and also for the piece of property in front of you.

Many business people are driven by a desire for money. They want bigger deals with more profit and there's nothing wrong with that. The desire purely for profit doesn't do it for me personally. That goal isn't my goal. For me, the goal is being excellent at my job and developing an amazing property. That's what I visualise and that's what pulls me forwards.

BE BOTH CONFORMIST AND ALSO LEARN TO STAND OUT

Some of the most successful people I have met have learnt to be both conformist and individual. This sounds like an oxymoron. Let me explain. Real estate is one of the oldest professions there is. There are certain rules of society and behaviour that you should conform to and, conversely, some rules that you don't need to bother with. In the UK, we are quite a conformist country and there are accepted norms and standards which are known and expected. It's certainly good to start from the proviso that you need to work out what the property industry wants and expects, and you should meet these expectations or you risk being judged negatively.

Nowhere is this more obvious than your choice of dress. The way you present yourself is the first thing people see of you and within the first few minutes of meeting you they have usually made their judgement about you, so it's good to get your first impressions right. Clothing and the way we dress is a very easy way for people to signal which "tribe" they belong to. It signals to others who they can relate to and trust.

A conservative approach to dress is usually the norm. Blue suit with no tie or chinos/jeans and a polo shirt are the investor's standard go-to uniform. I tend to wear slightly smarter clothes (a leftover from my lawyer days) and also a nod to the fact that we focus on the higher end of the market which has more of an emphasis on creativity and design that most developers lack. But I'm certainly not pitching up to meetings looking like Elton John.

There is actually a very big difference between knowing the rules, making a conscious and well-educated decision to break them, and just being clueless about the rules to start with. We have all seen well-dressed city guys wearing great suits and looking the part, with one stand-out thing that's different – for example, a bright tie or these days more likely a bright pair of socks – which expresses their individuality or just makes a point. The point being that they know how to behave but are deliberately choosing to wear something a bit out of the norm as they have the self-confidence to do so.

> ## Once you know the rules, you can deliberately break them.

Work out how to express your individuality and which rules and boundaries you can push or break. If you really want your personality to shine through, then you can do this. The best way to do this is to first focus on your work and strategically and very carefully review what image you would like to portray of yourself.

My day-to-day business aim is to create very well thought out properties with cutting-edge design quality using the very best building materials and absolutely the best builders. So I take the standard investor's uniform and I adapt it to reflect my work. All my suits and shirts are smart and tailored. I aim to keep myself in decent shape and generally consider I'm one of the better turned-out guys in the room. How I dress reflects the quality of work we are doing and sets me apart slightly from the crowd.

You have to be willing to bring attention to yourself and to promote your brand and properties.

POWER PRINCIPLE 40

STUDY THE COMPETITION

You should constantly be learning. I try to learn something new every day and one of the best sources of information and knowledge is your competition. You can see what mistakes they have made and also what good work they have done. Places like Manchester City Centre and London have some very experienced and well-funded developers and it's great fun and very beneficial to look at what they have done.

It's key to know what wavelength your competitors operate on and how they think. You can learn from them and if you can pre-empt what they will do, this will give you a competitive advantage.

There are many local networking events and online resources where investors communicate and get ideas from each other. I often have great conversations with other investors and developers and I am very willing to let others get ideas from me, while at the same time I am very keen to see what they are doing and what is working for them. It's my job to work out how I can improve on my performance and how I can, at the end of the day, do the best job and get the best profit for our properties.

> Spend a lot of time looking at what developers are doing with properties that are in a price range just above yours.

I spend a lot of time looking at what developers are doing with properties that are in a price range just above ours. Even though we wouldn't be able to reproduce some of the features they have done as they would be too costly, we can see what the next level up is doing and maybe pick a few of their ideas or do a cheaper version.

And if you see something that inspires you, then get out there and do it. Try new things that you have seen others making a success of. It's the doing that is all-important. Do, copy, work out what works for you and then improve it.

NEVER LOSE SIGHT OF THE PERSONAL SIDE OF A DEAL

Buying and selling real estate is a people game. If you possibly can, it is always best to meet the potential buyer or seller personally face-to-face and get a relationship established. You will encounter many problems that need to be solved during any transaction and it's easier to do this if you have a direct relationship with the other side. In fact, don't think of them as the other side, think of them as a partner in the transaction. You will both share some (although not all) of the same goals in actually getting the deal done and any help you can get along the way is worthwhile.

I've done deals that have fallen through for strange and just wrong reasons sometimes. Maybe some of these deals could have been salvaged if I had been able to work closer with the other side. I've also seen many, many situations where my good working relationship with the other side has been invaluable in solving issues that have occurred and has resulted in deals being pushed across the line where other people would not have been able to do the deal.

Recently, I was selling a flat to a 70-year-old lady, who was downsizing from her family home. She had exchanged on the property, but then when the time came to complete she was delaying, and the agent said she was having cold feet. Now, I had met her several times during the process, so I contacted her directly and asked what the problem was. It turned out that she thought the external stairs to the property were too steep for her and she was worried that she wouldn't be able to make it up and down them in a few years' time. After a lovely chat with her, we had agreed to install a hand-rail at the side of the steps. She was happy and we completed quickly after that.

Quite often, for logical reasons, the professionals involved will try to keep themselves between you and the buyer or seller. Lawyers and estate agents especially like to operate this way. While it's good from their perspective, it's not always the best thing for you and can add an extra layer to an already quite difficult conveyancing process. I find it's always best to get a direct channel of communication established between yourself and the other party as early on as you can. I will usually try to be there at any open days we have and will be handing my card out to any potential purchasers, so they can always contact me if they need to. If we do get a sale agreed, I usually ask the estate agent if I can have the buyer's details so that I can wish them congratulations and to be there to help if they have any questions about a property.

Try to get direct contact at the negotiation stage of the deal, right at the very start of the process.

KITCHENS SELL HOMES

Focus on the kitchen when renovating a property to sell. Kitchens sell homes. Investing in an amazing kitchen is definitely one of the best bangs for buck, you can get when spending money on a property. We sell and rent to millennials and the trend here is towards open-plan living. We don't have separate large kitchen/dining rooms in our properties. We usually combine the kitchen and living/dining room and create a well-designed open-plan environment. Our kitchen/living spaces are the most central parts of our properties, and this is where the "wow!" factor needs to be.

You really can't overestimate the importance of a sexy-looking kitchen and the title of this section is 100% correct: kitchens do sell homes. The kitchen is absolutely top of the heap when it comes to rooms of importance. Kitchens at the top, then living rooms, bathrooms then bedrooms. The kitchen is the most important room in the house. Even though we spend at least eight hours a day in the bedroom, it's the relatively few hours after work each night we spend in the kitchen/living room that is the big, heavy-hitting, important time in a person's life. This after-work oasis of happiness is what people tend to think about when buying a property.

Everyone aspires to have a great kitchen and to be the amazing host spending time in that kitchen. They will picture themselves entertaining and having a drink and some food with their suitably-impressed and happy friends. That's what our buyers want and we give them what they want, because they are the boss, after all.

We have always spent a disproportionate amount of money on the kitchen and it's been repaid ten-fold. We focus on the design of the kitchen and colour scheme. We have an interior designer designing our kitchens in addition to the normal "kitchen guy" from our supplier who measures up and designs the initial rough plan of the kitchen. We usually have the same-sized units next to each other and as many of the most modern touches as we can. Wine fridges, granite worktops, waterfall island units, dishwashers. We will try to fit in as much as we can.

> ## The kitchen should be neutral but should also give a "wow!" factor.

In fact, the kitchen should usually be the number one "wow!" factor in the flat. By neutral but "wow!", I mean that the kitchen must be extremely impressive, should not offend anyone and must appeal to everyone. Neutral and bland will not cut it, but neutral and "wow!" certainly will.

POWER PRINCIPLE 43

FIRST IMPRESSIONS COUNT

People make quick decisions mentally – in real estate, as in so many things, first impressions count. The online estate agency Emoov calculates that it takes the average person 65 minutes to decide whether to buy a home or not, and 30% of decisions are made within the first five minutes. This is not a lot of time considering the amount of money at stake and the importance of the transaction, so it's important to get the first impressions right.

By kerb appeal, I specifically mean what the potential buyer will see from the road, as soon as they get out of their car and look at the property for the first time. Create some good kerb appeal for your property: mow lawns/sweep any paths/ensure dustbins are emptied/paint the front door/get the windows cleaned. Do whatever needs doing.

The same principles apply when the potential buyer opens the front door to your property. You want them to be bowled over by it. Make sure it's well turned out, clean, well-dressed, the heating is on, there's a nice smell to it. Make it feel like a desirable home not a sterile box.

> **You never get a second chance to make a first impression.**

Usually, a person has made up their mind as to whether they want to buy your property in the first few minutes. And the clock starts ticking from when they enter your garden/driveway. So many developers miss a trick by only focusing on the interior of the property. However, by the time the key turns in the door, a lot of the decision-making has been done. You want to be impressing the buyer from the moment they first look at the property from the street.

Even if it isn't your responsibility, or if it doesn't belong to you, you need to make the surrounding area looks as good as it can be. If you are selling a flat in a block, make sure that the communal areas are well turned out and clean. Even if it's the management company's job not yours, why not vacuum the floor and tidy the post away if it will help you get a sale?

POWER PRINCIPLE 44

SELL THE SIZZLE: SELL THE LIFESTYLE

You should know your target market. Know their expectations, their needs and wants from a property. However, it's not just a property you're selling, it's a lifestyle. It's somewhere for someone to live and experience a certain lifestyle. First and foremost, they are buying a lifestyle and secondly, a property.

It's the lifestyle that they want and aspire to that they will be buying, not necessarily the lifestyle that they currently have.

> **People don't buy for logical reasons, they buy for emotional reasons.**

People buy with their heart and afterwards their head justifies the decision. Buying a home is about a feeling not a location. People like to feel rooted and to have a sense of belonging. At the end of the day, it's about the people not the property. When we are selling a property we want to create a feeling of being at home, of being happy and connected. Safety, security and comfort are three concepts that you should have firmly in your mind when working out what your target market wants. It's not always high-end fixtures and fittings. That can be too superficial. If it was, then everyone would be living in new-build swanky apartments in the city centres. Some people do, but a lot prefer our renovated Victorian properties.

Yes, the financials and the various metrics buyers use are important but, really, at the end of the day the buyer will only buy if they can visualise themselves living in and, importantly, enjoying the property. Can they see themselves finishing a hard day of work, coming home, cooking, having a glass of wine in an inspiring and safe environment, and generally having a great experience?

You need to sell the benefits of your property not just the features, fixtures and fittings. For example, emphasise the amazing natural light, spacious open-plan living area, great amenity space, a quiet street, proximity to shops, great views, pleasant neighbours, etc. Some people will be focused on nice restaurants and shops. Others will be focused on schools and toddler groups. It's important to know your target market and their needs and to emphasise the benefits of your property to them.

The cost per square foot of a property almost never sells a home. It's the sizzle that sells the bacon!

POWER PRINCIPLE 45

COPY AND IMPROVE ON A BUSINESS PLAN THAT WORKS

When I was setting up my business nearly 20 years ago, I met as many property investors, landlords and developers as I could and I studied what they were doing and what was working for them. I also studied what I could easily replicate but also improve upon.

One business plan that became one of the cornerstones of our future company was to buy the worst property on the street. An older, more established investor, already had this plan. He would buy the cheapest, nastiest building he could find and then would do it up to the standards of the other properties on the street in as cost-effective a way as possible. The other properties were all comparable and even if he didn't do a particularly amazing renovation job, it was still quite easy to significantly increase the value of his property by relying on the values of the surrounding properties. He was, in effect, surfing a wave and it was a good business plan. I copied this in the early years of our business and relentlessly viewed and bought some of the most disgusting properties you could imagine. We bought crack houses, prostitute haunts, houses and flats that were so disgusting that they weren't fit for animals to live in. I viewed them all. No property was too disgusting for us. In fact, as long as the street was alright then the worse the state the property was in, the better. We were going in to do a renovation on it anyway; the last thing I wanted to do was to pay extra for someone else's half-assed renovations.

This "buy cheap and renovate cheap" business plan worked well, but very quickly I realised that we could go one step further and turn the worst properties in the street into the best and get even more profit. As I already had the builders in doing the work, and labour was the most expensive part of the renovation and development process, why not employ a great interior designer, use a few better quality and better-looking materials and up the standard? For an extra 5% to 10% spend, we could increase the value by 30%.

It was unusual for professional investors to aim for the higher end of the market back then, and there wasn't actually much of a higher market, but I was sure that if I built it they would come.

We started small at first, just testing our business plan. We did a new type of kitchen tile here, a different paint colour there. It all worked, so we kept on going. Now, we get the best sales prices in our areas. We don't overspend. We need to justify that every £1 will be beneficial, is necessary, and will result in £1.20 in profits coming back to us.

We know what to spend to maximise our returns.

> **We took some risks and gambles in the early stages, but they were relatively small and calculated, and none of them would have sunk the business.**

This is a great way to beta test your product.

The bottom end and the top end of the market have some great opportunities. I have operated in both areas and they work well. In my view and experience, the middle of the market is harder to operate in and people tend to end up here by accident. Both the bottom of the market and the top of the market are very different places. They serve different clientele and I would definitely recommend that you think carefully about where you want to end up. It's good early on to really analyse your personality and strengths and weaknesses to see where your natural abilities are, and which end of the market you are best suited to working in.

If you are very focused on the bottom line and have quite a tough no-nonsense personality, then you could do well at the lower end of the market. If you are a flamboyant design-focused individual who loves pretty things around and has an overriding sense of style, then you will probably gravitate to the higher end of the market. When I have been successful, it's been because I've been focusing on the areas that are best suited to my skill set.

POWER PRINCIPLE 46

GO BIG AS SOON AS YOU ARE COMFORTABLE DOING SO

I started out buying, renovating and selling single, small apartments worth less than £100,000. After doing this for several years, I had cut my teeth and learned a lot. I realised that it would be a way better use of my time to step up a level and do larger deals. I saw an opportunity in blocks of flats in old, large properties and in the early days it was primarily the financial side that I was focused on. If I could do one deal worth £1,000,000, that would generate the same profit as 10 deals worth £100,000 all rolled in to one transaction, yet the time costs were pretty much the same. This was leverage at the extreme and I realised that this was the way forward; the way to leverage and supercharge results.

> When you do a larger transaction, it is pretty much the same amount of work as one small one.

You just need to imagine that there is an extra zero on the end of the contract. You still need one buyer, one seller, one estate agent, one surveyor, one contract, one mortgage. Most of the process is the same for a small deal as it is for a big deal and the amount of time involved is roughly the same as well.

When you get to the building side, then there are obviously extra costs and considerations involved. If you are renovating one 500 sq.ft. flat, it will obviously take less time than doing 10 of them. However doing 10 in one block, or just doing one large house that is 10 times as big (5,000 sq.ft.) doesn't take 10 times the amount of work. There will be huge economies of scale involved in doing a larger project.

You will be able to have one team in one set geographical location working away for a decent amount of time. Contrast this to having to do 10 separate flats spread out over several different areas. You would have to spend a lot of time arranging for the builders to travel between sites and all the increased logistics that these sites would entail. For example, it's far easier to get one plumber to lay the pipes for a whole building containing 10 flats, than it is to get that plumber to go round to 10 separate flats and do his work. Would you rather arrange for one delivery from your supplier to your one property or for 10 separate deliveries to 10 properties?

When you do step up a level from the "starter" properties, you find that you are out of the amateur game and playing with the professionals, and that's a very good thing. Most investors never get out of doing small and mid-range deals. Most investors in the UK actually own less than four properties. When you step up and start doing real developments then you start dealing with professionals and, if you know your stuff (as you should do by this time), this is actually great news for you.

When amateur investors apply for a mortgage, they usually have no real relationship with the bank, and they will either get the loan or they won't if they don't manage to tick all the boxes. When you start doing bigger deals the banks will want to meet you, see a business plan, and track what you are doing. Yes, you will need to be good but once you have proven yourself then you have a proper relationship with an individual or group of individuals at the bank. This makes doing business so much easier. I find there is very much a sweet spot once you get away from single deals, where you have access to better funding and support from the banks.

We have now developed over 500 homes and I can tell you that the best profit is made on the larger jobs. Go big as soon as you are comfortable doing so. This is the way to leverage up and really make some excess profit. Start small, test the market. Buy a cheap terraced house, renovate and learn from what you do. Then do larger transactions, larger still, and continue until you get to the level you want to be at.

POWER PRINCIPLE 47

CREATE A PERSONAL AND BUSINESS IMAGE THAT SETS YOU APART

Once you establish yourself as an investor and entrepreneur you will immediately start to develop a style and image, whether you want one or not. In the age of social media, now more than ever it is remarkably easy to develop and create an image and publicity for very little outlay. In short, you need to build a business and personal brand. It's always been important to generate publicity, but now it's free and easy. Social media has been a real game-changer for small businesses.

It's a necessary part of your business to create and promote your own personal and business brand, and if you are not skilled in self-promotion you need to read up on it. It's a serious skill in its own right.

You probably don't want to overdo it, but you definitely don't want to undersell yourself. If in doubt, it's better to lay it on a bit thick than risk putting nothing out there. Even if your content isn't the most interesting thing in the world, it's great to get some material out there so that you have a presence and you are portraying yourself as an established and serious investor. After all, one of the first things anyone does when considering doing business with you is to do an online social media search on you. Everyone from buyers to tenants to bank managers do this and it's good to have a well-considered and constructed business and personal image out there.

As well as using social media sites and posting yourself, it's even better if you can get other people to post about you. It's great if you can harness the power of the media and you certainly need to be thinking about how to appeal to reporters and journalists. There are many traditional reporters out there craving content, as well as a new breed of online bloggers, vloggers, influencers and podcast producers. If you have something that can help them write an article or contribute to a piece of an article; you will be doing them a favour.

Don't be embarrassed. You are allowed to be a little pushy and get your amazing business in the public domain. Part of your job now is to contact the media and get yourself and your message out there. Everyone will have a different message. Our message is that we are a high-end developer, operating in South Manchester, specialising in apartment blocks. We are a medium-sized business focusing on specific geographic and demographic niches. We have been in business for nearly 20 years and are very active investors. If anyone is considering doing a bit of due diligence on us, it will be very easy for them to see who we are and what we do. We don't need to send them a business plan. They just need to go to our website and social media pages.

Anything of positive value that sets you and your business apart from the competition is of benefit to you. Each time we build or renovate a house or apartment block, we will take photos of our work and put them online. If your work is good, take a photo and put it out there. If you don't, then how will people find out about you? We document all of our jobs. We have photos of the demo work, the structural work, electrics, plumbing, excavation and landscaping and especially the finished work.

My personal image is nothing too flash. I am not a person who naturally loves the limelight. Yes, I am a property developer and so by definition I have an ego, but I don't like to put myself out there on a two-dimensional level by just saying, "I'm great, look at me." So often, I see property people posting photos of themselves sitting drinking champagne in first-class lounges or on their latest holiday. I don't think that's good PR. It may be a bit of interesting eye candy for a few seconds, but it's too trivial and usually shows that someone is a wannabe rather than an expert. I prefer to make most of my social media and PR, stuff about the work we are doing. I like to post pictures of myself or my workers on site. I like to post pictures of our building work (pipe laying, kitchen finishes, brick cleaning, an oversized window, some great-looking tanking.

> **Tell the world why you are good and why people should be doing business with you.**

Focus on what sets you apart from others. It may be a bit of a quirk in your personality or it may be a type of work that you are doing. Yes, you do have to generally conform to recognised standards but if there is something unique and individual about you, something that sets you apart and will get you remembered, then that's a good thing.

One prominent Manchester developer quite often wears hats and pin-striped suits, which is a bit different in today's marketplace. It stands out and gets him noticed. He also backs it up by building some of the best properties in Manchester. He's created a personal image that people don't forget easily and his business brand is first rate. The two need to go hand in hand.

POWER PRINCIPLE 48

ALWAYS NEGOTIATE WIN-WIN DEALS

One of the earliest and best business books I read was *The Secrets of Power Negotiation by Roger Dawson*. It had a huge impact on my overall business style. The book starts from the premise that we are negotiating all day, every day, to get what we want and need and so it's good to learn the basics of how to negotiate and hence deal with people.

One of the main themes of the book, which really resonated with me, was the advantage of thinking with a win-win mindset. If you are doing business with someone then you are in effect constantly negotiating with them, each and every time you meet. If you can create a situation where both/all parties are happy with the result, then it's fair and reasonable, and not only will all parties want to ensure that the deal goes through, but they will want to do more business with you. It's pretty simple.

Back in 2008, during the Great Recession, we found ourselves in a situation where we couldn't purchase a property we wanted to and had agreed to purchase. The banks pulled all finance offers and basically closed for business in early 2008. With no bank finance available, I had to go back to the seller and explain that I couldn't purchase his property. We discussed the situation and it soon became clear that he didn't need the money immediately and that certainty of sale and money at some point in the near future were more important to him than a quick deal. Once we had established this, I was able to put a deal to him whereby he would in effect lend me the money to buy his property. No money would actually change hands, but he would go from being the legal owner to having a first charge on the property. I told him that I would then develop the property and I would then sell it and repay him the money. He even offered us a loan for the development costs, which we gladly took. He got a better return than he was originally expecting, and I managed to do the deal.

Most people think that master negotiators are the ones who can get the biggest discounts. Images of haggling to get the cheapest carpet in a Turkish bazaar spring to mind. This is only correct for one-off situations.

> **If you want to create great long-term relationships, as you should do, then aim to create situations where all parties are happy and clamouring to do business with you again.**

You don't want to be the patsy in the room, but you definitely need to leave some money on the table and ensure that everyone is making an acceptable profit.

POWER PRINCIPLE 49

TAKE CALCULATED RISKS

Profit can be defined as the reward for taking risks. Generally, the more adventurous you are with your business, and the more risks you are taking, the greater the potential rewards will be. Buying property, doing deals, expanding your business (in fact, most forms of action in the property world), are risky, but the more business you do and the more actions you take, the more profit you can achieve.

However taking risks and failing can lead to substantial losses, and you don't want to lose money do you? One school of thought says that you should avoid risk as much as possible. How can we as property developers – which, almost by definition is a high-risk profession – do this though? We encounter thousands of problems with every transaction and build we do. Taking risks and problem-solving is at the very heart of our core business plan and the reality is that you will be engaged in taking quite a lot of risks on a very regular basis if you are going to have a successful business.

The topic of risk-taking is very much a grey area and it is hard to give a precise answer as to how much risk you should be taking in your business. Often, people just have different risk profiles and some people are far happier dealing with risk that other people would find very uncomfortable. We all have certain predispositions for how much risk we feel comfortable taking. That's why some of us like sky-diving and others prefer reading books. But we can also train ourselves to get more comfortable with risk and we can also work hard to make situations that initially appear risky, less so.

Risk should not be viewed as scary and unpredictable. Risk is actually an opportunity. If you can grasp the opportunity and solve the problem, then you will be able to take the profit that others are just walking away from.

By doing your due diligence and fully understanding the details for your work, even the most complicated problem/risk can be rationalised, analysed and the complexities stripped away one by one, so it hopefully becomes a fairly simple issue to resolve. Look at the financials of a potential deal. What is the best that can happen, the normal, the worst? How much potential profit is there in a deal and how likely is it that you can get all of that? What do you need to do to get the profit? What are the downsides? What can you potentially lose?

At the end of the day, if you have done your due diligence and you still aren't sure, play safe and follow the "if in doubt, don't do it" principle.

Consistently analysing and dealing with risk is like working out in a gym. The more you work on your muscles in the gym the bigger and better they get, the less they hurt and the better results you get. Dealing with risk is just the same. You should be constantly looking at and analysing risks and then taking the acceptable ones. This process will lead you to become more comfortable taking risks. You need to flex your "risk muscle" on a very regular basis.

To fully succeed in life and a property career, you are going to have to take risks. So if you are risk tolerant, then it's best to start working hard and training yourself to work out how to take these risks.

ABOUT THE AUTHOR

Peter Armistead is a graduate of Durham University and the College of Law, York. He spent 6 years as a lawyer in a top City law firm and then in an investment management company, before leaving corporate life to set up a property business. He has been a professional property investor and developer for the last 18 years.

Peter is an innovator, an investor, an award-winning developer and a business owner. He has bought and sold several hundred properties. His business, Armistead Property, is one of the most prestigious property development businesses in South Manchester and specialises in renovating old, neglected properties and turning them into some of the finest properties in the area.

As well as having a passion for property, he is a highly accomplished skier and a competitive ultra mountain runner, having been on the podium for races at the 50k, 50-mile, 75-mile and 100-mile levels. He has worked in over 30 different countries and currently lives in Whistler, BC, where he works, skis and/or runs every day.